Written on Skin

–

The Opera Lively Guides volume 2

Luiz Gazzola

Publisher: Opera Lively Press
ISBN-13: 978-0692379714 (Opera Lively Press)
ISBN-10: 0692379711

Printed in the United States of America

See also from Opera Lively Press:

By the same author Luiz Gazzola:
"Opera Lively – The Interviews" volumes 1 and 2
"Les Troyens – The Opera Lively Guides" volume 1

By Jay Hunter Morris:
"Diary of a Redneck Opera Zinger"

DEDICATION

To Irene and Astolpho, who taught me everything,
and to George Benjamin, whose genius revitalized
opera.

George Benjamin – Photo Credit Opera Lively

Table of Contents

Preface...1
Chapter One - Genesis of the Opera 7
   Circumstances of Composition and Interview with
       George Benjamin...7
   George Benjamin - Biography 24
   Characters...30
   Synopsis...30
   The Full Text of the Opera 35
Chapter Two - The Literary Source.................................68
   Interview with Author Martin Crimp 71
Chapter Three - Around the Opera 75
   Some Trivia about Written on Skin.....................75
Chapter Four - The Music of Written on Skin 77
   Orchestration...77
   Scene-by-Scene Musical Commentary 79
Chapter Five - The Characters and their Voices 94
   Agnès...95
   The Protector 96
   The Boy 97
   The Two Comprimario Roles 98
Chapter Six - Discography...99
   Recordings in Audio and Video and Vocal Score.........99
   Audio (CD) 100
   Video (DVD, Blu-ray disc) 101
Chapter Seven - Singing and Acting in Written on Skin...104
   Interviews with Performers.................................104
   Barbara Hannigan 104
   Christopher Purves 124
   Tim Mead 134
   Tammy Coil 157
Chapter Eight - The Opera in the Opera House.............164
   Interview with Stage Director Katie Mitchell.............164
   Complete Performance History...........................170
   The World Premiere - Review 174
   The United States Premiere at Tanglewood 178
General Index...185

ACKNOWLEDGMENTS

Our thanks go first to the staff at Opera Lively Press, who provided advice and commentary at various points of the writing of this guide.

Special thanks go to George Benjamin's assistant Joni Hurst for arranging the interview with the composer and various other helpful actions; to Samantha Holderness from Albion Media for facilitating the interview with Barbara Hannigan; Matthew Horne from Intermusica for the Tim Mead interview; George Benjamin himself for the Christopher Purves interview; Nicola Biltoo from Julia Kreitman Agency for the Katie Mitchell interview, and Rozzy Wyatt from Judy Daish Associates for the Martin Crimp interview. Our thanks also go to Bruce McCrae from Faber Music, Ltd, for help with the authorization to use the text, the score, and the synopsis.

Many scholars and critics who wrote about *Written on Skin* before us also have our gratitude, since much of the information we are presenting here in guide format was found in their much more complete and thorough works.

And of course, we are most thankful to George Benjamin, for the legacy of this masterpiece, and the attention he granted to Opera Lively.

Preface

"*Written on Skin* - Opera's New Masterpiece - If opera is a dead art form, somebody forgot to tell George Benjamin." Mike Silverman, Associated Press

"Magic and irresistible… the best opera written over the last twenty years." Renaud Machard, Le Monde

"… feels like the work of a genius unleashed." Alex Ross, The New Yorker

"What can an opera do for us today? Very simple I think: move you… enchant… stir you… thrill you… just like four hundred years ago except we have to find new ways of doing it." George Benjamin, composer of *Written on Skin*

Opera Lively Press is presenting the second volume of its series of opera guides. Nothing could be more fitting than addressing *Written on Skin*, a towering masterpiece that took the operatic world by storm when it premiered in Aix-en-Provence in 2012. Unlike other contemporary operas, it rapidly got picked up by many major opera companies, and it continues to be performed. When it completes three years of existence in the summer of 2015, it will have clocked more performances in the same period than *Peter Grimes*. It is conquering a just place among the very best works of the operatic repertory. The opera won the first International Opera Award in the "World Premiere" category on 22 April 2013 in London. It was also the Editor's Choice for the BBC Music Magazine.

Based on an Occitan legend from the 13th century reported by the poet Guillem de Cabestaing (which has inspired Boccaccio and Stendhal as well), the opera tells the story of a love triangle, with a married woman engaging in an adulterous relationship. A wealthy lord brings into his house a young illustrator, from whom he commissions a book of illuminations to celebrate his political power and his position as chief of his household who dominates his obedient wife Agnes. However, she seduces the illustrator and makes him change the content of the book, in order to convey to her husband who she really is. Her husband then kills her lover and makes her eat part of his body (his heart, in a horrifying scene), which leads her to suicide.

Written on Skin is this writer's most favorite contemporary opera. Its compelling, high-quality text contains all elements one might ever expect from opera, with love and lust, loyalty and betrayal, jealousy, revenge, and violence, and all of this illustrated by gorgeous music.

It is a powerful work given its complexity and emotional impact. Performances have been extremely well received by audiences and critics alike, with many sold-out runs. It has staying stamina in the repertory, and it is sublime. This is what we intend to demonstrate with this guide.

STRUCTURE OF THIS GUIDE

The Opera Lively Guides Series in its volume 1 (*Les Troyens*), this volume 2, and all the upcoming volumes will follow a structure that begins with the Genesis of the Opera comprising an introduction to the circumstances of composition of a piece, the composer's biography, a list of characters, and a detailed synopsis. In the case of *Written on Skin*, we have included the complete text (what is usually called the libretto but Mr. Crimp prefers the word "text"), with its integral reproduction duly authorized by Faber Music, Ltd. Also, there is no one better to talk about circumstances of composition than the composer himself, and we had the pleasure of interviewing him in person. This interview is reproduced here in its entirety, and can be also found in "Opera Lively – The Interviews – Volume 2." We included an extensive commentary on Benjamin's and Crimp's first opera, the short (37') chamber work *Into the Little Hill*.

Next, we address the source for the work, comparing and contrasting works of art or historical events that have inspired the librettist and the composer. In the case of Written on Skin, this section also contains a text especially written for us by Martin Crimp.

The third division deals with what we call Around The Opera. It may contain trivia, interesting information about the opening night and subsequent runs, bits of odd facts related to the work, as well as major theories and essays about aspects of the piece. Given that *Written on Skin* has been around for only three years, this section in briefer in this guide than in our previous and likely our subsequent guides.

Next, we make comments on the music of the opera, including duly authorized illustrations of the vocal/piano score. This will then be followed by a division called The Characters and their Voices, where we describe voice types and singers who have tackled these roles. A discography with comments on the opera recordings in audio and video occupies the next division.

Then, in Singing and Acting, we print exclusive Opera Lively interviews with artists who have recently performed these roles – in the case of *Written on Skin*, we have the pleasure of sharing with our readers our interviews with Barbara Hannigan and Christopher Purves, the artists who created the main female lead role of Agnès and one of the two leading male roles of The Protector, and also Tim Mead who sings The Boy, and Tammy Coil, who sang the role of Marie in the opera's United States premiere in Tanglewood. These interviews address as well topics other than *Written on Skin*, and are of interest for all opera fans.

Finally, in the division called The Opera in the Opera House, we will address productions of the work with performance history, and it includes an exclusive interview with the original Stage Director Katie Mitchell.

A WORD ABOUT CITATIONS AND URLs

The present volume is a guide, not a scholarly work. Our intention is merely one of providing to readers a convenient compilation from various sources (program notes, liner notes, Internet sources, including our own previous online writings on this opera, written at the time without a preoccupation with citations). We aim at enhancing our readers' ability to appreciate this opera that we love, by making this information available to them in compact format. Thus, while we did include our own thoughts and insights in many points of this volume, we make no claim that this was always the case, since we did, as well, paraphrase and summarize the ideas of others, especially printed reviews of the work. Recovering these sources which in many case are ephemeral (such as a review that is published than removed when it gets old) is a rather impossible task, therefore we just apologize to the authors for using summaries of their thoughts without being able to specifically quote them.

We also indicated some URLs for Internet-based video clips. Given the changing nature of the Web, URLs may become outdated after this guide's press time, and if this is the case, we encourage readers to use search engines in order to get to similar video clips.

Luiz Gazzola, MD, PhD
Chief Editor, Opera Lively
February 2015

OPERA LIVELY ONLINE

If this book is your first contact with Opera Lively, we invite you to explore our online operations. You will find more than 160 exclusive interviews with the most prominent operatic artists, literally hundreds of original articles; exciting online opera-themed novels being published chapter by chapter; in-depth analyses of great operas including musical structure, discography, stagings, and trivia; a singer's section; reviews of CDs, DVDs, and Blu-ray discs; reviews of live performances and broadcasts; operatic news; classifieds; a very active discussion forum, and much more. It is a friendly and accessible place that welcomes beginners, but also includes comprehensive and expert-driven content that is informative and educational. In addition to the majority of articles and posts in English, there are small but growing sections in Spanish, Italian,

French, German, and Portuguese. The entirety of our content is made available to readers free of charge, and also free is registration as a member (necessary to post your own comments). You can find us at www.operalively.com.

Chapter One - Genesis of the Opera

Circumstances of Composition and Interview with George Benjamin

In one of our most interesting interviews to date - and fittingly, George Benjamin was our 100th interviewee - Opera Lively talked in July 2013 with the incredibly talented composer in anticipation of the US Premiere of his outstanding opera Written on Skin.

Opera Lively - I congratulate you on the incredible success of *Written on Skin* which has taken the opera world by storm. I confess that it is in my opinion one of the three best contemporary operas I know, and one of the top twenty overall of all time, in my preference. So, we'll be soon talking extensively about *Written on Skin*, but I'd like to start by asking you about your music, in general. I see its style as something that is a bit hard to pinpoint – you do seem to employ chromatic scales and pentatonic scales, and in the past you've used microtones [intervals smaller than a semitone], but sometimes you also seem to zoom into a note and sustain it for long periods. Please clarify for our readers what is your musical style, and whether or not you affiliate yourself with any sort of school or movement.

Luiz Gazzola and George Benjamin – photo credit Opera Lively

George Benjamin - I have used microtones in some of my pieces – quite a long time ago – but they are not a regular part of my technique. My music is not conventionally tonal or atonal, and indeed frequently poly-harmonic, and I'm afraid I don't have a simple label to describe it. I have never been a member of a movement or group, and have always valued independence above all things.

OL - I think that what is admirable in your music is that you are very clear, very transparent. There is an incredible purity of sound. You employ sometimes a large orchestra

– like in your *Written on Skin* with 60 instruments – but you seem to use each section of the orchestra sparsely and not simultaneously, so that while there is polyphony and lots of colorful texture, there are also moments of crystalline focus on one instrument, or of course when it's opera, on the voice, which seems to drive the harmonies and be the strongest core of the piece (which we, opera lovers, very much appreciate!). I believe that this is very efficient to tone-paint dramatic, strong, conflicting emotions. I know that this is too broad a question to ask, but maybe not. What would you say you try to express with your music?

GB - Quite simply I try to express or represent what the text demands – its narrative as well as its form. Transparency is frequently a major priority for me – I love the idea of a multi-faceted musical fabric where all elements are simultaneously perceptible, individually as well as in combination. In *Written on Skin* it was essential to me that the voices could sing softly and yet their lines – and the text – could be heard. And the way to achieve contrasts in color across a large structure is through omission – leaving an aural "vacuum" in the texture, and then filling it while preparing another one... So, just in terms of orchestration, the first loud high trumpet note in the opera appears 40 minutes into the structure; the glockenspiel has only one note in Part One; the glass harmonica is only used in two scenes in the whole work; high soft flutes are only used once, etc. And the same approach applies to below the musical surface and to the formal (and above all harmonic) elements.

OL - I listened to your *Dance Figures* and simply loved it. *Sometime Voices* was also very nice. I am eager to get to know more of your output. If a classical music consumer wanted to get acquainted with the very best pieces of George Benjamin, what would the man himself – you - advise him or her to get?

GB - Probably, I think, start with my two operas – *Written on Skin* and *Into the Little Hill*. *Dance Figures* is more accessible than some of my other works, and much simpler in form and expression; alternatively perhaps I might mention *Upon Silence*, *Three Inventions for chamber orchestra*, *Palimpsests* or *Shadowlines*.

OL - As we the Opera Lively staff listened to *Written on Skin*, one of us heard influences of Britten, Debussy, and Berg. I heard Sciarrino especially in the way that you elongate the vowels, and Debussy in terms of dreamy, hypnotic sounds from the orchestra – *Pelléas et Mélisande* comes to mind (not to forget that Mr. Crimp's libretto touches on relatively similar themes to those of Debussy's masterpiece). If not, who were the greatest influences on you? I know that you studied with Peter Gellhorn, Alexander Goehr, Robin Holloway, the great Olivier Messiaen, and Yvonne Loriod – and did you study with Pierre Boulez?

GB - He has been extremely important to me, though he wasn't my teacher.

OL - I know you are a fan of Ligeti. You have also mentioned at one point that Purcell and Webern were divisors of waters in your musical growth, and you've quoted Indian music as influential as well. So please tell us about the synthesis of these multiple influences you might perhaps feel your music has evolved into.

GB - The most important influences? Indeed, most of the composers you mention above (though not all!). Though there are probably some others as well.

OL - Every composer has their own process that works for them. Sometimes it is an earwig that catches in the mind from which major parts of the score are spun. What can you tell us about your own composition process? From where does it come?

GB - I have techniques though no fixed method. Composing always remains a challenge for me; every passage seems almost impossible at first, and somehow I find a way of realizing what is required. All I can say is that I sketch copiously and throw out 30 times more than I keep – and there is a lot more going on behind the scenes than sometimes seems the case.

OL - At the very young age of 16, you took lessons from Messiaen. Apparently, he compared your musical talents to those of Mozart. How did that come about, and how did you receive this evaluation from the great master? Did it place a burden on your shoulders?

GB - He was the most wonderful, devoted, enthusiastic, and inspiring teacher; I loved and revered him and I owe him more than I can ever express. Sometimes his enthusiasm, however, got carried away, and I never took that comparison to Mozart at all seriously...

OL - After a number of very well received instrumental pieces, you took upon yourself to compose a short opera, and then a full length opera. What brought you to the operatic art form? Can you please describe to us what is your relationship with opera, and how did it evolve over the years, from childhood into adulthood?

GB - I already wanted to write opera, even when a young child. I had a wonderful illustrated book of myths and fables, and would improvise operas to them in my head for hours on end. Then I sometimes accompanied silent movies on the piano as a student, and that taught me something about controlling large stretches of time as well as narrative pacing and intention. But the crucial element was, for me, the meeting with Martin Crimp – his style and his language inspired me and, quite simply, opened the curtains of musical theatre to me...

OL - Let's address your fist opera, *Into the Little Hill*. It is really surprising, how you and Mr. Crimp got a traditional story like that of the Pied Piper of Hamelin, and packed so much in 37 minutes. How did the idea of setting this to music come about?

GB - It was one of the 50 subjects I suggested to Martin when we first agreed to collaborate – a list that I had been preparing for decades. The Pied Piper was there because I had already started an opera on that subject when about 14, with text by a school friend. (It was terrible, by the way, and fortunately never got beyond the first appearance of the rats...)

OL - The Stranger – the Pied Piper character in your opera - says that music opens the door to the heart, and that music stops death. One would say it's a direct quote of how powerful music is. Was this a particular intention of this piece?

GB - Yes absolutely, one of its main themes.

OL - Why did you employ two female voices – a soprano and a contralto – to sing each, multiple characters?

GB - Economy of means above all; though I perhaps also have a slight preference for high voices. And the wonderful singers for whom I conceived the work – Anu Komsi and Hilary Summers - inspired me.

OL - Any particular reason for not having an overture, and starting the first bars with the piercing shouts "kill, kill"?

GB - Yes, immersing the audience into the drama immediately, without any comfortable or engaging instrumental preparation.

OL - *Into the Little Hill* was very well received. Did the motivation to write a full-length opera come from its success?

GB - Yes, of course, though it had been an ambition, as I mentioned before, since my beginnings as a composer.

OL - Did you expect when you composed *Written on Skin* that it would be so well received by critics and audiences alike?

GB - I never began to imagine the response it has received...

OL - How did you get to collaborate with Martin Crimp? I know you met him in 2005 after looking extensively for someone to write for you an opera libretto. Other than being an incredibly talented playwright, he is also a pianist – did this latter aspect help in terms of your operatic collaboration?

GB - A mutual friend – the distinguished American violist and scholar, Laurence Dreyfus – introduced us. Martin is an extraordinary writer and yes, his intense musicality is also immensely helpful for our work together.

OL - Who picked the story that was the source for *Written on Skin*, you or Mr. Crimp? How was the process of selecting the theme for the opera?

GB - Martin's eldest daughter Catherine was responsible for finding the precise Occitan story on which the opera is based – though it was the director of the Aix festival,

Bernard Foccroulle, who encouraged us to look in that direction. The work, indeed, owes an untold amount to him.

OL - What aspects of this 13th century story inspired you to compose an opera? Some will say it's a feminist theme with this strong heroine Agnès.

GB - The story is simple, strong and dramatic. It deals with big, universal themes. But it was Agnes' response to her husband's gruesome crime which was the deciding factor – her defiance is in the original text, and I believe it remains powerful and startling even today.

OL - Did Martin Crimp write the entire text before you started on the musical composition, or was it a collaborative effort?

GB - We met and talked endlessly before he wrote the text, though I didn't start composing till Martin's task was complete.

OL - Your music is incredibly atmospheric, at times sensual, even erotic, at other times urgent and powerful complementing the dark actions and words of the libretto. The ups and downs of this powerful story are admirably rendered by your music, employing for instances static periods of tension, then shocking, furious orchestration when things get hectic. How did you proceed to create this incredible match? Line by line with, or in broader painting strokes?

GB - Both, at the same time! I had to be aware of the sonorous implications of every word in the text, while constantly trying to shape and control musical construction on the largest scale. Both are essential, I believe – though the fusion is far from easy. It's like simultaneously looking through a microscope and at a distant alpine landscape, if that's not too picturesque or banal an analogy...

OL - Let's address a little bit your use of two great instruments that are rarely seen in opera: the viol or viola da gamba, and the glass harmonica. First, the viola da gamba, which you contrast with cellos and basses and low trumpets, trombones and horns. What did you want to express with this arrangement?

GB - The viol is only used in scenes 6 and 15, two moments of great importance in the story. Its melancholy and sensual tones add, I hope, a new timbral dimension to the work at these junctures. I also wanted to coat the instrument's sound in unusual timbres, in particular medium-low brass played fortissimo with practice mutes – mutes by which very strong playing becomes soft and seems apparently distant. A by-product of these mutes played loudly (the force employed is still clearly audible) is an expansion of harmonics, in a way not too far from the viol's own generous spectrum – hence I believe they combine well, creating a spangled overall sonority.

OL - Now, the glass harmonica. I simply love it. One of my favorite operas is *Die Frau ohne Schatten*, and it uses it. I also feel that the productions of *Lucia di Lammermoor* that do use it in the mad scene like Donizetti intended, get to be much more haunting and beautiful than those that use a flute, instead. So please tell us about how you utilized this fabulous instrument in *Written on Skin*.

GB - The instrument has fascinated me for years, though I never used it before. I love the way one can hear the friction between the fingers and the glass; the resultant sound is simultaneously extremely resonant and yet highly fragile. It's also a wonderful harmonic resource and I have written some pretty complex chords for it (up to 10 notes!). It's also used in only scenes 6 and 15, like the viol, so it's reserved exclusively for these two important moments. The Boy is an illuminator, and I imagined these instruments as the most special hues he could use...

OL - The narrative technique in the third person – where the characters talk about the action before they perform it, and refer to themselves as The Protector, The Boy, and The Woman, is very powerful, besides functioning like a sort of meta-language about the operatic art form itself, with its artificiality – people don't talk to each other by singing while in opera they do, so this narrative form introduces an element of theatre within the theatre that is very interesting for opera. This is Mr. Crimp's hallmark style, since his play Attempts on Her Life. This, coupled with the role of the Angels in moving events along, made me feel that the opera addresses the inevitable destiny of the characters, like a train wreck in the making that can't be stopped, given the human condition. Would you agree? If not, how would you define the function of this particular narrative structure?

GB - You have expressed it very well, thank you. The place of opera in our culture has changed – a lot – since the 19th century and both Martin and I felt impelled to address the challenge of how to make the form feel natural in the 21st century. The auto-narration we have used is one response to that crucial issue. This very simple convention, paradoxically, allows me to be more spontaneous and direct than would have been the case with a more conventional text. Plus, for me, it also provides moments of strange poetry which lift the work into the realm of dreams.

OL - This might be more a question for Mr. Crimp but I guess you're also fully equipped to address it. Some of the text evokes downright macabre imagery. For example, the Protector's line, "Take his hair in your fist - says the third - pull his head back for a kiss: and as you are cutting one long clean incision through the bone, examine your own portrait in the glass-black mirror of his eyes." This is also a great example of the juxtaposition of sensuality and death imagery in this opera--for example here, of one man sensually kissing another as he draws the knife through the other's abdomen, looking in his eyes. Any comments on Mr. Crimp's powerful text, and its imaginative and concise use of language?

GB - Quite simply his language, as well as his unique sense of structure, inspires me; it's as simple as that! Plus he is the most generous of collaborators, and I do feel that he plants his texts with the specific words and imagery that will most directly provoke my music.

OL - In both *Into the Little Hill* and *Written on Skin*, there are anachronistic elements – the limousines in the first one; the references to an international airport in the second one, etc. The interplay of past and present is very interesting in the libretto. For example, when The Boy is talking about the future and says, "I'm thinking that when, when this wood and this light are cut through by eight lanes of poured concrete, I'm thinking that the two of us and everyone we love, everyone, will have been dead for a thousand years." This particular staging by Ms. Katie Mitchell is definitely looking back at this medieval story from contemporary times. Were you trying to get at how perennial these human dramas are?

GB - Yes, absolutely- plus the alluring strangeness of juxtaposing distant history with today.

OL - The opera seems to progress at a hectic pace through the setting up of the situation in Part One, with growing tension and an explosion of eroticism to end it; then, a very disrupted and fragmented Part Two where all the emotions are in turmoil; then we get to the lyric, ponderous, almost serene Part Three where the damage has been done and now it's a question of letting it all take its course (well rendered by Katie Mitchell in the slow-motion final scene). One would say that an essential characteristic of *Written in Skin* is it harmonic motion. It also doesn't seem to employ leitmotifs – there is always novelty as it goes on, making for a very rich score. How do you describe the musical structure of your opera?

GB - There is definitely something in what you say; in particular the scene after The Boy's murder in Part Three where – before Agnes's final aria - the music does somewhat retreat from the heat of the narrative in order to let the drama take its inexorable course.

There are no conventional leitmotifs, though there are leit-harmonies and leit-timbres, if you will allow me to employ those terms! And yes, harmonic motion is extremely important, an absolutely crucial resource in the construction of form on this scale.

You say "always novelty"? Yes, exactly – I wanted, until the last bar, to continuously introduce fresh and unexpected elements into the work's sound-field, in tandem with the drama and its evolution.

OL - Those that have seen the world premiere will by now have tied the three main roles to Bejun Mehta, Barbara Hannigan, and Christopher Purves, not to forget the excellent comprimarios Victoria Simmonds and Allan Clayton. You worked very closely with them during the composition and it can be said that they created the roles. Tell us about the collaborative process with the singers.

GB - All five of the singers came to my home, and I accompanied them in lieder and took copious and detailed notes of their precise vocal capacities. I had their voices in mind throughout the process of composing, and their vocal idiosyncrasies directly shaped the vocal lines I wrote.

OL - How much input did they have to give regarding the vocal lines?

GB - Nothing regarding the precise notes themselves; but the lines were conceived directly into their voices, which are therefore – in a way – present in every single bar of the score.

OL - How has it been to work with other singers on the roles which you created for your original singers? Have you had to modify the score or vocal lines in any way to accommodate different singers?

GB - No accommodations have been necessary – and, of course, it's fascinating for me to hear others perform the roles, though nothing will ever erase my memories of the original cast and their extraordinary performances.

OL - The Aix-en-Provence Festival production was extremely powerful. For example, when Purvis embraces Mehta and sings of telling Agnes of The Boy's betrayal with Marie. Was it as you had envisioned in your mind's eye as you composed the work or where there new elements which Katie Mitchell surprised you with? How closely did you work with Katie on the world premiere staging? We've interviewed stage directors before, and they said that when they are staging a work by a living composer, some of them feel it's the composer's baby, and they feel that they must respect the composer's artistic vision. Some others said the composers stepped back and let them develop their own vision. Who had artistic control over the world premiere?

GB - Katie's work was superb and yes, she surprised me with many things – it's an authentic production of the work after all, something I'm not really sufficiently skilled or experienced to envisage myself. And yet Martin and I worked very closely with her before and throughout rehearsals, and she remained absolutely loyal to our vision for the piece.

OL - Now that you have seen *Written on Skin* staged, are you satisfied that it succeeds dramatically as you imagined while you were composing it? Is there anything you would change?

GB - Probably not, though I'm too close to judge... But the work is complete, out in print (my excellent publisher has already produced the vocal and full scores) so even if I wanted to change it now it's not possible.

OL - We are about to have the US premiere of *Written on Skin*, conducted by yourself, at the Tanglewood Festival on August 12, 2013. What are your expectations for this performance?

GB - I love Tanglewood – I think this is my sixth visit since 1999 – and I hugely look forward to working with the gifted young musicians there in the wonderful Ozawa Hall, in that exceptionally beautiful landscape.

OL - Are you at a liberty to tell us about future plans for having the opera fully staged in America? We do know of the upcoming European runs up to this 2013-2014 season – your opera has achieved runs by 8 different companies in 13 months which is utterly remarkable for contemporary opera – so, you don't need to tell us about what is already happening, but we'd be curious to know about the future.

What else is in the horizon?

GB - There are several more new productions confirmed over the next few years, plus continuing revivals of the original one. There are also advanced plans for fully staged performances in the USA, though it's too early for me to be specific. [Editor's note: See the Staging/Performance History chapter for details, which now at press time are available]

OL - You have quite a talent for dramatic tone painting. Would you like to explore other genres, such as lighter, comedic opera?

GB - I love comedy, but am not entirely convinced by the comic potential of music – at least my own music. Though I do love *Gianni Schicchi*; let's see in due course...

OL - Your next commission is scheduled for 2018, which is five years out. How did you schedule this? Are there other projects you will be working on in the meantime, or it's just because opera houses these days are all booked up for the next several years? Are you at a liberty to tell us a bit about this commission? Have you already thought of a theme?

GB - Sorry, both Martin and I are highly secretive about our work, so my lips have to remain sealed. Though neither of us work fast, so five years isn't excessive...

OL - Sometimes contemporary opera with its emphasis on drama and, for the non-initiated, its less melodic, more fragmented music, has an uphill battle to win the hearts and minds of traditional opera lovers. But how would you go about this uphill battle, in terms of conquering an audience? I mean, you've done it already, given that the Royal Opera House shows of *Written on Skin* sold out, so you may have some insight to share with us in terms of getting other pieces to be as successful – besides, obviously, having talented composers like yourself at the helm. Is there something that can be done to better familiarize the public with the language of contemporary opera? I feel that in mainstream media classical pieces of other eras are given a lot of exposure, but contemporary music is not.

GB - Write from the heart, try to understand theatre, take risks with the form and take nothing for granted, and above all love the human voice and its interface with instruments – that would be my immediate advice.

But I am encouraged, it has to be said, in the seemingly huge interest in modern opera that has emerged in recent years here in the UK and across Europe.

OL - I'd say, in America as well, there is strong interest in contemporary opera, and we at Opera Lively do our best to cover it. Do you follow the work of other contemporary composers?

GB - Yes, a lot – in particular for my conducting and teaching work.

OL - What colleagues of yours do you admire?

GB - From approximately my own generation: Oliver Knussen, Tristan Murail, Hans Abrahamsen, Unsuk Chin, Simon Holt, Julian Anderson... And amongst young composers that really interest me (including some of my own students) I might mention names like Luke Bedford, Sean Shepherd, Saed Haddad, Vasco Mendonca, Dai Fujikura, Martin Suckling, Christian Mason...

OL - Teaching seems to be one of your passions. Tell us

about today's students of composition, especially those who want to focus on opera. In this day and age of worldwide economic crisis and budget constraints for the high arts, what advice do you give to your young students who want to embrace a career in composition?

GB - I can't usually advise them about their careers, but I can try to help with their compositional technique and clarity of vision. There is much interest in new opera here in the UK, and, though limited, there are resources which young composers can approach for experiment and research in this field.

OL - Your partner Michael Waldman is a filmmaker. Are there plans to get into scores for the movies?

GB - No plans for movie music! Though I do love film as a medium its musical potential, alas, usually seems distinctly limited.

OL - Let's end if you don't mind by asking you about the person underneath the artist. What are some of your extra-musical interests?

GB - Literature, art, cinema, landscape, my extended family and friends, tennis...

OL - What kind of person are you, in terms of personality?

GB - For that, you would need to ask Michael!

OL – Thank you for a great interview!

GB – Thank you!

George Benjamin - Biography

George Benjamin was born in London, United Kingdom, on January 31, 1960. He attended Westminster School, and then went to Paris in the mid 70's, where he was the favorite pupil of the great composer Olivier Messiaen at the Paris Conservatoire. Back to England, he studied at King's College, Cambridge, under Alexander Goehr, and became the youngest student to have a piece performed at the Proms, in 1980 (*Ringed by the Flat Horizon*).

Many other great pieces followed. Here is a list of George Benjamin's selected works, among others:

Ringed by the Flat Horizon (1979-80) for orchestra

A Mind of Winter (1982) for chamber ensemble

At First Light (1982) for chamber ensemble

Jubilation (1985) for orchestra and mixed children's group

Antara (1985-87) for 2 flutes, 2 computerized keyboards and ensemble

Upon Silence (1990) for mezzo-soprano and 5 viols or 2 violas, 3 cellos and 2 double basses

Sudden Time (1989-93) for orchestra

Three Inventions (1993-95) for chamber orchestra

Sometime Voices (1996) for baritone solo, chorus, and orchestra

Palimpsests (1998-2002) for orchestra

Dance Figures (2004) Nine choreography scenes for orchestra

Into the Little Hill (2006) A lyric tale for soprano, contralto, and ensemble (chamber opera)

Duet (2008) for piano and orchestra

George Benjamin received honors and accolades: he is a Commander of the Order of the British Empire, a Chevalier dans l'Ordre des Arts et Lettres, and a member of the Bavarian Academy of Fine Arts. He was awarded the 2001 Arnold Schönberg Prize, and the Deutsche Symphonie Orchester's 2002 Schoenberg Prize for Composition.

In addition to being a celebrated composer, George Benjamin has had important conducting activity, appearing regularly with the London Sinfonietta, Ensemble Modern, the Cleveland and Concertgebouw orchestras, the Berlin Philharmonic and the Junge Deutsche Philharmonie. Not only he conducts his own works, but he has conducted *Pelléas et Mélisande* at La Monnaie in Brussels, and numerous world premieres and important works by Wolfgang Rihm, Unsuk Chin, Grisey and Ligeti.

Given that Opera Lively is primarily interested in opera, we will review in more detail George Benjamin's other operatic work:

Into the Little Hill (2006), a lyric tale in two parts, sung in English

Music by George Benjamin.
Libretto by Martin Crimp.

Nimbus Records CD - NI 5828, DDD, one CD

Ensemble Modern, conducted by Franck Ollu

Cast
Anu Komsi, soprano, in the roles of The Crowd, The Stranger, Narrator, and The Minister's Child

Hilary Summers, contralto, in the roles of The Crowd, Narrator, The Minister, and The Minister's Wife

Recorded on November 9 through November 11, 2007, at the Bockenheimer Depot, Frankfurt Opera

Producer Udo Wüstendörfer - a co-production with the BBC and Hessian State Radio (Hessischer Rundfunk Frankfurt). Balance Engineer Thomas Eschler

Running time 37 minutes

The insert contains the full text of the libretto, and various essays, all in English.

Also on this CD, two other pieces by Benjamin:

Dance Figures (2004), Nine Choreographic scenes for orchestra - running time 16 minutes

BBC Symphony Orchestra conducted by Oliver Knussen, recorded at the Barbican, London, on March 29, 2008 (Commissioned by La Monnaie, The Chicago Symphony, and Strasbourg Musica)

Sometime Voices (1996) - running time 10 minutes
Deutsches Symphonie-Orchester Berlin conducted by Kent Nagano
Rundfunkchor Berlin
Dietrich Henschel, baritone
Recorded live at the Philharmonie, Berlin, on February 13, 2005

This is the acclaimed contemporary composer George Benjamin's first opera - a chamber piece for two voices and fifteen instruments (horns, cornets, flute, clarinet, trombone, cimbalom, strings - which includes a mandolin and a banjo in addition to violins, violas, cellos, and double bass).

This short piece which would be a great choice for a double bill, already hints at the greatness of *Written on Skin*. The plot is simple, and is the Pied Piper story. Brilliant British playwright Martin Crimp delivers a poetic text that is of rare intensity for its length. One wouldn't expect this simple tale to be this dramatic, but it is. The story is updated to more modern times, with limousines and politicians, and functions as an allegory of societal cast divisions between the rulers and the undesirable (the rats).

The power of music is celebrated in the piece. The Stranger says: "With music I can open a heart / as easily as you can open a door / and reach right in."

This is fitting, because Mr. Benjamin's music does just that. He is a master of dramatic tone painting. His vocal lines with elongated vowels (he reminds me of Sciarrino) are very efficient to convey mood states such as despair, dread, and fear, and get to be very touching. This is exemplified very early - couldn't get any earlier than this since there is no overture - given that the first sounds we hear when the opera opens, are shouts of "kill, kill." In spite of the harshness of the vocal lines (which do get to be lyric at times), the overall feeling is hypnotic, given the extreme beauty of the sounds coming from the instruments. Just like in *Written in Skin*, Mr. Benjamin's music envelops the listener in a sort of dream-like state (and now he reminds me of Debussy).

The two singers pass the difficult coloratura and the intense vocal demands with flying colors. Both do an excellent job.

I'd say that it is hard to pack so much, and so many interesting elements, in an opera that lasts for only 37 minutes - and Mr. Benjamin and Mr. Crimp did it!

The other two pieces on this CD are also great. I particularly loved *Dance Figures*, which is a study in contrast, made of an alternation of short and harsh segments with a bit longer and very melodious ones. *Sometime Voices* is also very compelling, and is well sung by Mr. Henschel.

After listening to these three short pieces by Mr. Benjamin and his longer opera *Written on Skin*, I'm a fan for life. I look forward to his new opera that has just been commissioned by the Royal Opera House, and will continue to explore his non-operatic music as well. We are in the presence of an extremely talented composer!

This CD is highly recommended, A+, for lovers of contemporary music. Available on Amazon.com for $18.21, and on the Amazon Marketplace for $10.47

Performance History for *Into the Little Hill*

The opera has had 70 performances in these places, in order of least to most recent: Opéra Bastille, Paris, France (premiere, Festival d'Automne, November 22, 2006); Saint-Quentin en Yvelines, France; Amsterdam, Nederland; Lincoln Center, New York City, USA; Frankfurt, Germany; Dresden, Germany; Birkenhead, United Kingdom; Vienna, Austria; Lucerne, Switzerland; Milan, Italy; Royal Opera House, London, United Kingdom; Oxford, United Kingdom; Leeds, United Kingdom; Prague, Czech Republic; Snape, United Kingdom; Buxton, United Kingdom; Gran Teatro del Liceu, Barcelona, Spain; Hamburg, Germany; Schwaz, Austria; Atalante, Göteborg, Sweden; Beijing, China; Sundsvall, Sweden; Umea, Sweden; Haparanda, Sweden; Wigmore Hall, London, United Kingdom; Birmingham, United Kingdom; Lisbon, Portugal; Briançon, France; Eveleigh, Australia; Budapest, Hungary; and Essen, Germany.

It is scheduled for 12 more performances in Stuttgart, Germany (Kammertheater) in June and July of 2015.

.

Now, back to *Written on Skin*.

Characters

Agnès (soprano) – Medieval housewife

The Protector (bass-baritone) – Agnès' husband, powerful landowner

The Boy (countertenor) – illuminator, hired by The Protector to paint the illustrated book of his family history

Comprimarios

Marie (mezzo-soprano) – Agnès' sister
John (tenor) – Marie's husband
Angel 1 (counter-tenor) – 21st Century angel and commentator
Angel 2 (mezzo-soprano) – same
Angel 3 (tenor) – same

Marie and Angel 2; John and Angel 3; and The Boy and Angel 1 are supposed to be sung by the same singers; therefore only five singers are needed, instead of eight.

Synopsis

This official synopsis by the author of the text himself, Martin Crimp, was generously sent to us by Faber Music, Ltd, and its reproduction was authorized.

PART ONE

I Chorus of Angels

"Erase the Saturday car-park from the market place —fade out the living — snap back the dead to life".

A Chorus of Angels take us back 800 years, to a time when every book is a precious object "written on skin". They bring to life two of the story's protagonists: the Protector, a wealthy and intelligent landowner "addicted to purity and violence", and his obedient wife — his "property" — Agnès. One of the angels then transforms into the third protagonist — "the Boy" — an illuminator of manuscripts.

II The Protector, Agnès and the Boy

In front of his wife, the Protector asks the Boy to celebrate his life and good deeds in an illuminated book. It should show his enemies in Hell, and his own family in Paradise. As proof of his skill the Boy shows the Protector a flattering miniature of a rich and merciful man. Agnès distrusts the Boy and is suspicious of the making of pictures, but the Protector over-rules her and instructs her to welcome him into their house.

III Chorus of Angels

The Angels evoke the brutality of the biblical creation story — "invent man and drown him", "bulldoze him screaming into a pit" — and its hostility to women — "invent her / strip her / blame her for everything".

IV Agnès and the Boy

Without telling her husband, Agnès goes to the Boy's workshop to find out "how a book is made". The Boy shows her a miniature of Eve, but she laughs at it. She challenges the Boy to make a picture of a 'real' woman, like herself — a woman with precise and recognizable features

— a woman that he, the Boy, could sexually desire.

V The Protector and the visitors — John and Marie

As winter comes, the Protector broods about a change in his wife's behavior. She hardly talks or eats, has started to turn her back to him in bed and pretends to be asleep — but he knows she's awake and can hear her eyelashes "scrape the pillow / like an insect". When Agnès' sister Marie arrives with her husband John, she questions the enterprise of the book, and in particular the wisdom of inviting a strange Boy to eat at the family table with Agnès. The Protector emphatically defends both Boy and book, and threatens to exclude John and Marie from his property.

VI Agnès and the Boy

The same night, when Agnès is alone, the Boy slips into her room to show her the picture she asked for. At first she claims not to know what he means, but soon recognizes that the painted image of a sleepless woman in bed is a portrait of herself, her naked limbs tangled with the covers. As they examine the picture together, the sexual tension grows until Agnès offers herself to the Boy.

PART TWO

VII The Protector's bad dream.

The Protector dreams not only that his people are rebelling against the expense of the book, but also, more disturbingly, that there are rumors of a secret page — "wet like a woman's mouth" — where Agnès is shown "gripping the Boy in a secret bed".

VIII The Protector and Agnès

The Protector wakes up from the dream and reaches out for his wife. She, however, is standing at the window watching black smoke in the distance, as the Protector's men burn enemy villages. She asks her husband to touch and kiss her — but he's disgusted at being approached in this way by his wife and repels her, saying that only her childishness can excuse her behavior. She angrily refuses to accept the label "child" — and tells him that if he wants to know the truth about her, he should go to the Boy: "Ask him what I am".

IX The Protector and the Boy

The Protector finds the Boy in the wood "looking at his own reflection in the blade of a knife". He demands to know the name of the woman who "screams and sweats with you / in a secret bed" — is it Agnès? The Boy, not wanting to betray Agnès, tells the Protector that he is sleeping with Agnès' sister, Marie — and conjures up an absurd scene of Marie's erotic fantasies. The Protector is happy to believe the Boy, and reports back to Agnès that the Boy is sleeping with "that whore your sister".

X Agnès and the Boy

Believing that what her husband said is true, Agnès furiously accuses the Boy of betraying her. He explains he lied to protect her — but this only makes her angrier: it wasn't to protect her, it was to protect himself. If he truly loves her then he should have the courage to tell the truth — and at the same time punish her husband for treating her like a child. She demands that the Boy — as proof of his fidelity — creates a new, shocking image which will destroy her husband's complacency once and for all.

PART THREE

XI The Protector, Agnès, and the Boy

The Boy shows the Protector and Agnès some pages from
the completed book, a sequence of atrocities which make
the Protector increasingly impatient to see Paradise. The
Boy is surprised: he claims that these are indeed pictures of
Paradise here on earth — doesn't the Protector recognize
his own family and property? Agnès then asks to be shown
Hell. The Boy gives her a page of writing. This frustrates
Agnès because, as a woman, she hasn't been taught to
read. But the Boy goes, leaving Agnès and her husband
alone with the "secret page".

XII The Protector and Agnès

The Protector reads aloud the page of writing. In it the
Boy describes in sensuous detail his relationship with
Agnès. For the Protector, this is devastating, but for Agnès
it's confirmation that the Boy has done exactly as she
asked. Excited and fascinated by the writing, indifferent to
his distress, she asks her husband to show her "the word
for love".

XIII Chorus of Angels and The Protector

The Angels evoke the cruelty of a god who creates man
out of dust only to fill his mind with conflicting desires,
and "make him ashamed to be human". Torn between
mercy and violence the Protector goes back to the wood,
and — "cutting one long clean incision through the bone"
— murders the Boy.

XIV The Protector, Agnès and the Angels

The Protector attempts to reassert control over Agnès. She

is told what to say, what she may or may not call herself —
and, sitting at a long dining-table, is forced to eat the meal
set in front of her to prove her "obedience". The
Protector repeatedly asks her how the food tastes and is
infuriated by her insistence that the meal tastes good. He
then reveals that she has eaten the Boy's heart. Far from
breaking her will, this provokes a defiant outburst in which
Agnès claims that no possible act of violence — "not if
you strip me to the bone with acid" — will ever take the
taste of the Boy's heart out of her mouth.

XV The Boy / Angel 1

The Boy reappears as an Angel to present one final
picture: in it, the Protector takes a knife to kill Agnès, but
she prefers to take her own life by jumping from the
balcony. The picture shows her as a falling figure forever
suspended by the illuminator in the night sky, while three
small angels painted in the margin turn to meet the
viewer's gaze.

The Full Text of the Opera

Mr. Martin Crimp prefers that we refer to his work as the
text of the opera, rather than as the libretto. The integral
work is reproduced here, as authorized by the original
publishers (see copyright notice on the first page of this
guide). **Paragraph and word positions are intentional.**

WRITTEN ON SKIN

Opera in Three Parts

Text for music by MARTIN CRIMP

After the anonymous 13th century razo GUILLEM DE
CABESTANH – *Le cœur mangé*

Set to music by GEORGE BENJAMIN

TEXT FOR MUSIC

Commande du Festival d'Aix-en-Provence,
De Nederlandse Opera (Amsterdam),
Théâtre du Capitole (Toulouse),
Royal Opera House Covent Garden London,
Teatro del Maggio Musicale Fiorentino

The composer and writer would like to express their
gratitude to Bernard Foccroulle, general director of the
Festival d'Aix-en-Provence, for his support throughout the
gestation and composition of this work.

PART ONE

I CHORUS OF ANGELS

ANGELS 2 + 3   Strip the cities of brick, dismantle
them. Strip out the wires and cover the land with
grass.

ANGEL 2   Force chrome and aluminium back into

the earth.

ANGEL 3   Cancel all flights from the international airport

ANGELS 2 + 3   and people the sky with angels.

ANGEL 1   Erase the Saturday car-park from the market-place. Rub out the white lines.

ANGELS 2 + 3   Shatter the printing-press. Make each new book a precious object written on skin.

ANGEL 1   Make way for the wild primrose and slow torture of criminals. Fade out the living: snap back the dead to life.

AGNÈS and the PROTECTOR are revealed/enter.

ANGEL 2   The woman?

ANGEL 1   Was married age fourteen.
               Can't write. Not taught to read.
               Grey eyed. Intelligent. No children.

ANGEL 3   And the man?
               And the man?

ANGEL 1   The man is her husband and protector. Calm. Powerful. Addicted to purity and violence.

ANGEL 1, transformed into the BOY, enters the action.

II THE PROTECTOR, THE BOY AND AGNÈS

PROTECTOR   Stand here. Look.

My house is perfect.
At night stars wheel over my vines
according to the strict mechanism
of the world.
And by day
– says the Protector –
fruit-trees, blue heads of iris,
pink cups of eglantine turn to the sun.

I own the fields:
I own everyone in them.
Every beech, each visible oak
is as much my property as my dog
my mill-stream
or my wife's body
– her still and obedient body –
is my property.

Make me a book.
Fill it with illumination.
Paint me the life to come
paint deeds of angels:
show me graves opening
the damned shoveled into ovens
and the just – us – us – my family – the pure
          and just –
show us in our rightful place:
show us in Paradise.

BOY   A book costs money, says the Boy.

PROTECTOR   I'll give you money.

BOY   A book needs long days of light.

PROTECTOR   I'll give you money. I'll give you light.
          But first: show me proof.

BOY   The Boy takes from his satchel
an illuminated page.

(FIRST MINIATURE: A WORK OF MERCY)

This – says the Boy – shows a Work of Mercy:
here – look – three men – all starving –
two wheeling on this cart the third.
And here's a rich man – see him? –
in a red satin coat lined with green.
In his face
round his eyes
see his expression
as he offers the three sick men wine and bread:
not just kind – explains the Boy – kind is too
        easy –
but merciful.

AGNÈS   No! says the woman.
Nobody here starves.
Nobody here begs.
What does this Boy want?
What does this thing this picture mean?

PROTECTOR But the Protector takes the page
gently to the window
looks deeper and deeper into the page –
recognises in the rich and merciful painted man
himself.
Says to his wife:
His talent's clear. I'm satisfied.
You will welcome him into our house.

III CHORUS OF ANGELS

ANGEL 2   Stone the Jew:

make him wear yellow.

ANGEL 3　　Crusade against the Moslem:
　　　　　map out new territory with blood.

ANGEL 2　　Invent the world.

ANGEL 3　　In seven days invent the whole world.

ANGEL 2　　Invent . . .

ANGEL 3　　　　　　　　　in a single day . . .

ANGEL 2　　　　　　　　　　　　　sun –

ANGEL 3　　moon – man –

ANGEL 2　　Invent man and drown him.

ANGEL 3　　　　　　　　　　　Good.

ANGEL 2　　Burn him alive.

ANGEL 3　　　　　　　　　　　Good.

ANGEL 2　　Bulldoze him screaming into a pit.

ANGEL 3　　　　　　　　　　　Good.

ANGEL 2　　Invent a woman.

ANGEL 3　　Invent her.
　　Strip her.
　　Dress her. Strip her again.

ANGEL 2　　Take her naked out of the toy-box.
　　Play house with her.

ANGEL 3   Play families. Play birth and death. Blame
        her.

ANGEL 2   Blame her for everything.
        Blame her mouth.
        Blame her intelligence.

ANGEL 3   Tint her flesh with a soft brush.
        Make her curious.

IV AGNÈS AND THE BOY

AGNÈS   The woman takes off her shoes
                            steps
        through a stone slit
                            turns
        up the spiral stairs
                            pads
        into the writing-room
        where the Boy
                            ah
                            yes
                            look
        the Boy bends over a new page.
        What is it she feels between her bare feet
        and the wood floor?
        Grit.

BOY   What d'you want, says the Boy.

AGNÈS   To see, says the woman.

BOY   See what?

AGNÈS   To see – to see how a book is made.
        What is that tree?

BOY   The Tree, says the Boy, of Life.

AGNÈS   Ah. Odd.

BOY   I invented it.

AGNÈS   Ah. Yes. And who is this woman?

BOY   Eve, says the Boy.

AGNÈS   Ah.

BOY   Yes.

AGNÈS   Invented too?

BOY   Yes, says the Boy, invented too.

AGNÈS   She doesn't look real, laughs the woman:
           that's not how a woman looks.

BOY   You're in my light, says the Boy.

AGNÈS   Oh?

BOY   Yes – too close.

AGNÈS   Oh? Too close in what way?

BOY   Too close to the page – you're in my light.

AGNÈS   What else can you invent?
           Can you invent another woman, says the woman,
           not this, but a woman who's real
           a woman who can't sleep
           who keeps turning her white pillow
           over and over

> from the hot side to the cold side
> until the cold side's hot?
> Can you invent that?

BOY   What is it you mean, says the Boy.

AGNÈS   And if the woman said, says the woman.

BOY   If the woman said what, says the Boy.

AGNÈS   Said – said – said –
what if you invented a woman
who said that she couldn't sleep –
who said that her heart split and shook
at the sight of a boy
the way light in a bowl of water
splits and shakes on a garden wall –
who said that her grey eyes
at the sight of a boy
turn black with love.

BOY   What boy? – says the Boy –

AGNÈS   You can decide what boy –

BOY   – what love?

AGNÈS   You can decide what love. Invent her –
invent the woman you want:
and when you know the colour of her eyes
her length of hair
the precise music of her voice –
when you've quickened her pulse
entered her mind
tightened her skin over her back
when you have invented and painted
that exact woman

•

come to me
show her to me:
I'll tell you if she's real.

V   THE PROTECTOR AND THE VISITORS – JOHN AND MARIE

PROTECTOR   The Archer appears in the sky:
the grapes are picked and crushed.
The Protector inhales the wine
watches hot blood from a pig's throat
spatter the snow at his visitors' feet –
thinks: my wife has changed –
won't eat – won't speak to me –
resents and avoids the Boy –

ANGEL 2 appears as MARIE, ANGEL 3 as her husband JOHN.

MARIE   How are you, says Marie.

PROTECTOR   – turns away from me in bed pretends –

MARIE   How is my sister, says Marie.

PROTECTOR   – to be sleeping
but in the dark her eyes are wide open
and all night
I hear her eyelashes scrape the pillow
                    click
                    click
like an insect.

MARIE   How is my sister?

PROTECTOR   My wife? – my wife is well.

Sweet and clean. Soft, still, obedient.

MARIE   And your house?

PROTECTOR   Increasing in value daily:
             nobody starves – everyone freely obeys.

MARIE   And the book?

JOHN   Yes – how's the book?
             Still eating money?

PROTECTOR   The book will be magnificent:
             the Boy
             works with azurite and gold.
             Both Boy and book are faultless.

JOHN   Ah. Faultless.

PROTECTOR   The Boy – yes –

JOHN   Ah.

PROTECTOR   – is faultless.

MARIE   The Boy is faultless?

JOHN   Don't, Marie.

PROTECTOR   The Boy is – yes – yes – yes – is faultless.

MARIE   What kind of man pays –
             pays to keep a boy like that in his own house?

JOHN   Be quiet, Marie.

MARIE   What kind of man sits a stranger next to

        his own wife
        at his own table?

PROTECTOR Listen to me: I love the Boy.
        Anybody who faults the Boy faults me.

MARIE   Nobody is faultless.

PROTECTOR   Do not fault the book, John.

MARIE   Nobody on this earth is faultless.

PROTECTOR   Do not fault the Boy, Marie
        or you will not pass
        the black dog at my gate.

VI AGNÈS AND THE BOY

AGNÈS   Woman – alone – night.
        Her visitors?
        Gone.
        Her husband?
        Sleeping in front of the kitchen fire.

        What can she hear inside of her?
        Her own voice.
        What does the voice want?
        To wind and to wind itself around another.
        Who does she catch
        click shut the black rectangle of the door?

BOY   Him. The Boy.

AGNÈS   What d'you want, says the woman.

BOY   To show you the page, says the Boy.

AGNÈS   What page?

BOY   Here.

AGNÈS   It's dark.

BOY   Then concentrate.

(SECOND MINIATURE: A HOUSE IN WINTER)

> This – says the Boy – shows a house in winter:
> here – look – white stars – Orion –
> and in this wide blank space, the moon.
> See how I've lifted the roof
> like a jewel-box lid.
> Inside's the woman – see her? –
> unable to sleep: buried in the hot white pillow
> her head feels heavy
> like stone.
> Round her legs
> round her arms
> I've twisted a lead-white sheet
> like a living person –
> and tightened her skin, darkened her veins with
>   blood.
> This is the woman's picture. Now you must tell
> me
> whether it's real.

AGNÈS   It's dark.

BOY   Then look more closely: what colour are her eyes?

AGNÈS   Grey – turning black – like my eyes now.

BOY   Like yours now.
    And her hair? Pay attention.

AGNÈS   Dark – damp – heavy – the weight of
        mine now.

BOY   Of your hair now.
        And her mind?

AGNÈS   You've given her my mind – skin –
        mouth –
                voice –

BOY   I've given her your mind – skin – mouth
        – voice –
                – says the Boy –

AGNÈS   – drawn its exact music.

BOY   – drawn its exact music.
        And here
        under the bone –

AGNÈS   No.

BOY   in the hot space between her ribs –

AGNÈS   No.

BOY   I've painted the woman's heart.

AGNÈS   No! – not 'the woman' – I am Agnès.
        My name's Agnès.

BOY   Agnès.

AGNÈS   What use to me is a picture?

BOY   Agnès.

AGNÈS   A picture – says Agnès – is nothing.
        Love's not a picture: love is an act.

END OF PART ONE

PART TWO

VII THE PROTECTOR'S BAD DREAM

ANGELS 2 + 3   People are saying –

PROTECTOR   People are saying what?

ANGELS 2 + 3   Saying the book eats –

PROTECTOR   Saying the book eats what?

ANGELS 2 + 3   TIME – CORN – RENT.
        Say it's a crow
        eating the seed
        making the people –

PROTECTOR   What?

ANGELS 2 + 3   TALK – LAUGH – STARVE.
        Not just the book –
        say that the Boy –

PROTECTOR   Say that the Boy what?

ANGELS 2 + 3   DRAWS – FROM – LIFE.
        Say there's a page
        where the skin never dries –

PROTECTOR   Page where the what?

ANGELS 2 + 3   SKIN – STAYS – DAMP.

ANGEL 2   Wet like the white
        part of an egg –

ANGEL 3   Wet like a woman's mouth –
        wet where a woman screams shrieks
        shrieks like a fox
        shrieks in the night in a secret bed.

ANGEL 2   Licking her lips
        flicking her tongue
        gripping the Boy in a secret bed.

ANGELS 2 + 3   What kind of man WILL – NOT
    – SEE?

                    What kind of man WILL – NOT
    – SEE?

VIII THE PROTECTOR AND AGNÈS

PROTECTOR   The Protector wakes up
        feels in the half-light
        for the reassurance of a human body –
        puts out his hand to be reassured by a human
            body –
        feels for his wife –
        Where is she?

AGNÈS   Here – smiles Agnès – I'm here by the
        window.
        You were thrashing in your sleep. Why?

PROTECTOR   What is it you're watching?

AGNÈS   Nothing. Sunrise. Plum-trees flowering.
               And smoke – why that black smoke in May?

PROTECTOR   We're burning villages.

AGNÈS   Ah. Why?

PROTECTOR   To protect the family.

AGNÈS   Ah. Yes. Good. From what?

PROTECTOR   Don't look.

AGNÈS   And in the meadow I saw a guard reach
               down into the buttercups to pick up a baby –

PROTECTOR   Don't look, Agnès.

AGNÈS   – to pick it up – how odd – on the point
               of a stick. Oh and I saw the Boy out riding into
               the wood like a picture out of his own book.

               Touch me.
               Kiss me.
               Take my head in your hands.

PROTECTOR   Don't be a child Agnès

AGNÈS   Grip my hair in your fist. Yes.
               Put your fingers into my mouth. Yes. Your
               tongue into my mouth now. Yes. Kiss me.

PROTECTOR   Only a child, Agnès, asks for a kiss.

AGNÈS   I'm not a child – don't call me a child.

PROTECTOR   No pure woman asks for a kiss.

> No clean woman asks to be touched.
> You are. You are a child, Agnès – say it.

AGNÈS   Don't call me a child –

PROTECTOR You're a child – say it.

AGNÈS   I refuse to be called a child.

PROTECTOR I said to you say it.

AGNÈS   No.

PROTECTOR Say it.

AGNÈS   No.

PROTECTOR You will say to me 'I am a child'.

AGNÈS   Ask him what I am.

PROTECTOR Say 'I am a child', Agnès.

AGNÈS   Ask him what I am. Go to the wood. Ask
           him –

PROTECTOR Ask who?

AGNÈS   – the one who writes on skin – ask him
           what I am – the Boy.

IX THE PROTECTOR AND THE BOY

PROTECTOR He finds the Boy
           sitting against a tree
           looking at his own reflection

> in the blade of a knife.
> Love-sick, thinks the Protector,
> easy to strangle – like a girl.
> What're you doing here?

BOY   Nothing.

PROTECTOR   What is it you're looking at?

BOY   Nothing, says the Boy,
thumbing the knife.

PROTECTOR   Thinking about?

BOY   I'm thinking that when this wood and this light
are cut through by eight lanes of poured concrete,
I'm thinking that the two of us
and everyone we love
will have been dead for a thousand years.

PROTECTOR   The future's easy: tell me about now.

BOY   Now there's just one slit
of pink light cut in the sky.

PROTECTOR   Tell me about now.

BOY   Now there's just you me
and a knife.

PROTECTOR   Tell me about now:
who is this woman? –
the one they say –
taunt me and say screams out
from a secret page –
says screams and sweats with you
in a secret bed?

What is her name?

BOY   I thought you trusted me.

PROTECTOR   What is her name?

BOY   I thought you loved me and protected me.

PROTECTOR   What is this woman's name? Is it Agnès?
Is what? Her name is what?

BOY   Not Agnès – no no no no no no no – Marie –
her name's Marie – Marie: her sister.
Look at her.

ANGEL 2 appears again as MARIE, ANGEL 3 as her
husband JOHN. MARIE is putting on a zip-up party
dress.

She came to me. She was bored. She wanted
to be Venus.

MARIE   I'm bored. I want to be Venus. Put me in
the book. Illuminate me.

As JOHN zips up the dress:

AH! THAT HURTS!

JOHN Sorry.

BOY   Then she wanted to be an angel. She wanted to
crank the universe round on its axis.

MARIE   Make me an angel. Give me power. I
want to control the universe.

BOY   Her marriage was banal. She longed for excitement.

MARIE   How do I look?

JOHN   We're late.

MARIE   THEN GET ME MY SHOES!

JOHN produces a pair of shoes.

NOT THOSE – THE RED ONES!

BOY   She volunteered to be Greed and Luxury – was happy to let me draw from life sick acts of perversity.

MARIE   Feed me pomegranates and soft-cooked eggs –   roast meat for me and drown me in wine and cream – wash me in goat-milk – strip me – dress me – strip me again – toss me naked into the toy-box. Draw my mouth as a scarlet thread. Shame me – chain me – drag me to hell. Shut me in eternal darkness with the devil. I'm ready!

JOHN   I don't want to hear. I don't want to know. Let's go, Marie. We're late – we're going to be late – let's go. We're going to be late, let's go, let's go, let's go.

JOHN and MARIE leave.

PROTECTOR   And her husband? –

BOY   – was complicit.

PROTECTOR   Is this the truth? Is this the truth?

BOY   Oh yes – believe me – it's the truth.

PROTECTOR And since this is what the man – this man
so much needed to believe – so he – the man –
this man – believed it

     And that same evening tells his wife – entertains
her – reveals – ha! – how – secretly – the Boy
enjoys – guess – guess – guess – that whore her
sister – yes! – and how that other man – that fool
the husband – smiles the Protector – is complicit.

X AGNÈS AND THE BOY

AGNÈS   Agnès puts on her shoes

                             steps
    through the stone slit

                             turns
    up the stone stairs

                             slips
    into the writing-room
    where the Boy

                             him
                             yes
                             the liar
                             look
    lifts his head –

BOY   Why are you crying?

AGNÈS   You lied to me.

BOY   In what way lied?

AGNÈS   All night your voice in my head
    wound itself round and around and around

         and around
my sister.
Her mouth fastened to yours
in a bad dream
and her hair stuck –
stuck like gold-leaf to your skin in a bad dream
and covered your eyes.

BOY   What dream?

AGNÈS   My sister – you – the liar – you and my
sister.

BOY   I lied for you, not to you.

AGNÈS   Prove it.

BOY   I lied to protect you.

AGNÈS   Protect – protect – protect:
to protect me or to protect yourself?

BOY   This isn't true.

AGNÈS   Prove it.
Let him see.
Show him us.

BOY   Show him us how?

AGNÈS   Or do you love him too?
Do you fasten your mouth
to his mouth too and bite –
bite on his lip like you bite on mine?

BOY   What is it – says the Boy – you want from me?

AGNÈS   While the dead heap up in the meadow
                while human beings burn in the market-
place make a new page:

> Push our love into that man's eye
> like a hot needle.
> Blind him with it.
> Make him cry blood.

END OF PART TWO

PART THREE

XI THE PROTECTOR, AGNÈS AND THE BOY

A long table is spread with pages from the
completed book. The BOY moves along the table
explaining the pictures.

BOY   Here are your enemies
       lined up on a gibbet.

PROTECTOR Hanging – excellent – like Judas.

BOY   A vine-hook
       cutting a traitor's throat.

PROTECTOR Yes yes – and who are these?

BOY   These naked boys have dug their own graves –
       they're waiting in an orchard to be shot.

PROTECTOR And what are these streaks of light?

BOY   A night bombardment:

Gomorrah – see it? – being turned to dust.

PROTECTOR   Yes yes, I see it – now show me Paradise.

BOY   An aquamarine flash –
streets running with human fat –

PROTECTOR   I see it – but show me Paradise.

BOY   A carmine flame licking a field of wheat –

PROTECTOR   I SAID NOW SHOW ME PARADISE.

BOY   Ah – ah – ah – no – yes – what? – Paradise?
But this is Paradise.
Here is your mill
and here are your cherry trees.
Here's – look – Marie shopping in the
shopping-mall
and John at the airport collecting air-miles.
This is Paradise.
These are its concrete walls.
And here – with a diamond skull –
the black dog at its gate.

AGNÈS   If this is Paradise – says Agnès –
then where is Hell?

BOY   Here – smiles the Boy – it's on this secret page.

AGNÈS takes the page and looks at it.

AGNÈS   Where are the pictures?

BOY   They're here: I've painted them with words.

AGNÈS   What words?

BOY   Read them.

AGNÈS   Read? Read? How can a woman read?
        What words?
        Is this a word?
        Or this? – this? – this? – or this?
        Where does a word end and another word begin?
        Where are the pictures?
        What use to a woman is a word?

BOY   The book is finished.
        My work – smiles the Boy – is done.

        The BOY goes.

XII THE PROTECTOR AND AGNÈS

The PROTECTOR examines the page in silence,
        then begins to read it to AGNÈS.

PROTECTOR mouth

                – see it –

    mouth

                – writes the Boy –
    heart hair mouth nail hand skin blood – her neck
                – writes the Boy –
    of amethyst, her long white back,
    even the gold-flecked iris of her eye:
    each part
    each part
    each part of her body
                – writes the Boy –
    she has offered and has used for her own pleasure.
    Like the man
                – writes the Boy –
    like the man who bends down the branch

in summer
to cut the most high-up flower
                            – writes – writes the Boy –
I have reached up for her love
and have bent her willingly to the ground.
And at her invitation
her own invitation
                            – writes the Boy –
we have used and used and used and used
have used each other as
                            – writes the Boy –
pornography.
This
is what the woman
what Agnès
what your wife your property
                            – writes the Boy –
what your wife your property
asks me to say to you.

AGNÈS   Ah.
               Read it – oh read it again.

PROTECTOR Keep away.

AGNÈS   And show me –

PROTECTOR Keep away.

AGNÈS   Please show me –

PROTECTOR Keep away.

AGNÈS   I want to see.

PROTECTOR Cover your arms.
               Cover your face and hair.

Stitch shut your lips before your pink pink
        flicking tongue
snakes back into my mouth the way it burrowed
        into his.
NOW KEEP AWAY FROM ME.

AGNÈS   Ah ah ah ah ah ah oh please please
        oh please let me see the word for love.

XIII CHORUS OF ANGELS AND THE PROTECTOR

ANGELS 2 + 3   Set the earth spinning –
        fill it with iron and stone.

ANGEL 3   Make a man out of dust.

ANGEL 2   Good.

ANGEL 3   Prop him naked on two stick legs.

ANGEL 2   Good.

ANGEL 3   Prop him tottering next to a tree.

ANGEL 2   Good.

ANGELS 2 + 3   Tempt him, taunt him, clothe
        him, spit him out.

PROTECTOR Expel him from joy
        with a lacerating whip.
        Make him sweat, cry,
        scratch at the earth's crust.

ANGEL 3   Make him jealous – make him ashamed.

PROTECTOR Make each man ashamed – yes – to be
human.

PROTECTOR + ANGELS 2 + 3
Put voices into his mind.

ANGEL 3   Confront the Boy

– says one –

follow him into the wood.

ANGEL 2   No

– says another voice –

be wise, be calm, be merciful.

PROTECTOR Take his hair in your fist
– says the third –
pull his head back for a kiss:
and as you are cutting one long clean incision
through the bone
examine your own portrait
in the glass-black mirror of his eyes.

(INTERLUDE: THE WOOD, MURDER)

XIV THE PROTECTOR AND AGNÈS

AGNÈS sits at a long table. In front of her, a metal dish.

PROTECTOR Woman and her Protector – night.
A room. A balcony. A long white table.
What has he placed in front of her?
What has he placed in front of her?

AGNÈS   A silver dish.

PROTECTOR   What does she lift from the silver dish?
      I said what does she lift from the silver dish?

AGNÈS   The warm round silver lid.

PROTECTOR   What does the woman do now?
      I said what does the woman do now?

AGNÈS   I'm not the woman: I'm Agnès.

PROTECTOR   I said what does the woman do now?

AGNÈS   Eats.

PROTECTOR   Good. Say it.

AGNÈS   The woman eats.

PROTECTOR   What makes the woman eat?
      I said what makes the woman eat?

AGNÈS   Hunger. Appetite. Her curiosity.

PROTECTOR   No: her obedience.

AGNÈS   Ah.

PROTECTOR   Her obedience.

AGNÈS   Ah.

PROTECTOR   Say it.
      I said to you say it.

AGNÈS   Her obedience now makes her eat.

PROTECTOR   Her obedience to her husband – that is

correct –
now makes her eat.

How does it taste – says the man.

AGNÈS   Good, she says – salt and sweet. Why?

PROTECTOR   Good?

AGNÈS   Yes, she says – good, she says – salt
        strange   and sweet. Why?

PROTECTOR   Good? How is it good?

AGNÈS   Sweet as my own milk, yes – good – but
salt – salt as my own tears. Why?

PROTECTOR   Good? How is it good?

AGNÈS   Why? What has my husband my
Protector given me to eat?

PROTECTOR   His heart, Agnès.

AGNÈS   What heart?

PROTECTOR   His heart – the Boy.

AGNÈS   No.

PROTECTOR   His heart – the Boy –

AGNÈS   No – no – nothing –

PROTECTOR   – his heart – his heart –

AGNÈS   Nothing you can do –

PROTECTOR – the Boy – his heart –

AGNÈS   Nothing I ever eat
        nothing I drink
        will ever take the taste of that Boy's heart
        out of this body.

        No force you use
        nothing you forbid
        can take away the pictures that Boy's hands
        draw on this skin.

        He can unfold the tight green bud
        unwrap the tree, darken the wood,
        lighten the sky, blacken the dust
        with rain – each mark he makes on me is good
        – each colour clear –

        Crush.
        Burn.
        Break.
        Tear.
        Put out my eyes.

        Hang.
        Drown.
        Stone.
        Stab.
        Cut out my tongue.

        Nothing
        nothing
        – not if you strip me to the bone with acid –
        will ever take the taste of that Boy's heart
        out of this mouth.

XV ANGEL 1

(THIRD MINIATURE: THE WOMAN FALLING)

The BOY reappears as ANGEL 1.

ANGEL 1   This – says the Angel – shows the
          Woman Falling:
          here – look – the man takes a knife
          but the woman's quicker, and jumps.
          See how her body has dropped
          from the balcony –
          how I pause her mid-fall –
          at the exact centre of the page.
          Here in the night sky – see them –
          stars hold in a bright web
          her black silhouette
          on blue.
          As she drops from the house
          three small angels – look –
          are watching her calmly
          from the margin.
          In their face
          in their eyes
          see their cold fascination
          with human disaster
          as they turn from the falling woman to where
          the white lines of the Saturday car-park cover
          the heaped-up dead.

END OF PART THREE

Chapter Two - The Literary Source

The opera is inspired by a brief legendary tale regarding the life of Guillem de Cabestany (1162–1212), who was a Catalan troubadour from Cabestany in the County of Roussillon in Southern France. He is also known by his Old Occitan name, Guilhem de Cabestaing, Cabestang, Cabestan, or Cabestanh.

According to his legendary *vida* (an Occitan literary form), he was the lover of Seremonda (or Soremonda), wife of Raimon of Castel Rossillon. On discovering this, Raimon fed Cabestanh's heart to Seremonda. When he told her what she had eaten, she threw herself from the window to her death. This legend appears later in Giovanni Boccaccio's *Decameron* and in the *Cantos* of Ezra Pound. Cabestany is presented as the archetypal troubadour in Ford Madox Ford's book *Provence*.

Martin Crimp changed slightly the story: The Boy, the character in the opera who corresponds to Guillem de Cabestany, became in the opera an illuminator rather than a troubadour, and is also younger – given that the historical character lived for 50 years.

MARTIN CRIMP'S BIOGRAPHY

Martin Andrew Crimp was born on February 14, 1956, in Dartford, Kent, United Kingdom. He is a highly celebrated, innovative, and prolific playwright.

His plays include *Three Attempted Acts* (1985), *Dealing with Clair* (1988), *Play with Repeats* (1989), *No One Sees the Video* (1991), *Getting Attention* (1992), *The Treatment* (1993, winner of the John Whiting Award), *Attempts on her Life* (1997), *The Country* (2000), *Face to the Wall* (2002), *Cruel and Tender* (2004), *Fewer Emergencies* (2005), *The City* (2008), and *In the Republic of Happiness* (2012).

He is also very active as a translator, of works by Molière, Ionesco, Genet, Marivaux, Chekhov, Bruckner, and others.

The son of John Crimp, a British Rail signaling engineer, and his wife Jennie, Crimp's family moved in 1960 to Streatham where he attended a local primary school before winning a scholarship to Dulwich College. But when his father was transferred to York, he went to the nearby Pocklington School, where he showed an aptitude for languages, music, English literature and theatre. He studied English at St Catharine's College, Cambridge, in the class of 1975–78. He became writer-in-residence at the Royal Court Theatre in 1997.

His most famous and highly regarded play, *Attempts on Her Life*, has been translated into twenty languages. It is a rollercoaster of late 20th-century obsessions. From pornography and ethnic violence, to terrorism and unprotected sex, its strange array of nameless characters attempt to invent the perfect story to encapsulate our time.

'Martin Crimp's coolly European meditation in 17 scenes on a woman, also called Anne - who may be a terrorist on the run, or an artist who has turned her suicide attempts into her art, or a traveler who has her photo taken by millionaires' swimming pools and in slums, or a woman whose children have been slaughtered in civil war, or even a child herself - is not an easy text for any director.' – Lyn Gardner – The Guardian

His work in the UK has been produced by the Orange Tree Theatre, the West Yorkshire Playhouse, the Stephen Joseph Theatre, the RSC, the Young Vic and the Royal Court, where he was writer-in-residence in 1997. In New York his work has been seen at the Public Theater and the Classic Stage Company, as well as on Broadway.

Martin Crimp's style is appropriately dry, in the fact that nothing is superfluous and dialogues are restrained and precise, with some emotional detachment like if a social scientist or psychologist is studying the character – the theatrical language is what seems to interest him as a sort of metalanguage, instead of a linear narration structure. In Crimp's works, relationships are not very successful. His characters struggle with bitterness and lack of love or happiness.

His works have been described as elliptical, indirect, austere, and they demand concentration. He aims at avoiding familiar forms of theatrical expression. Instead, his plays engage audiences in ideas relating to the commercialization of daily life, the artist's consumption by the entertainment industry, the inherent violence in domestic environments, the restrictiveness of social class, and the understanding of a nation's own identity through its encounter with the Other.

Benjamin said of Crimp's text in an interview to the Boston Globe published in the August 10, 2013 issue, by journalist David Weininger: "I believe that opera today has to acknowledge that we live the era of film, and as a result naturalistic drama is full of pitfalls and dangers for the lyric stage. On the other hand I believe that storytelling is still essential. Martin invented the auto-narration technique for his plays, and it was the first thing that appealed to me about his style. In a very simple way it enables us to acknowledge the artificiality of the operatic medium, and then bypass it; I cannot imagine writing music to scenes of such highly charged eroticism or brutality if the style of speech were everyday. . . . This convention — plus the juxtaposition of eras — makes the whole tale feel as if it were in a dream world; that also, I think, beckons the type of music I can write."

Interview with Author Martin Crimp

Opera Lively sent interview questions to Martin Crimp. He took care of writing his answers as a continuous piece of prose. Here are some of the questions we sent him, followed by his text (questions by Luiz Gazzola for Opera Lively):

Written on Skin is undoubtedly a smashing and almost unprecedented success as far as contemporary opera goes, thanks in no small measure to your outstanding text, as well as to Mr. Benjamin's fabulous music. Were you expecting such an impact?

How do you compare the constraints (or maybe the advantages) of producing text for music versus text for spoken theater?

Is the sonority of specific words more important in the operatic art form, and did you adapt or adjust your poetic writing to this aspect?

Please describe the creative process while working with the composer.

Please talk to us about the selection of the medieval story that inspired *Written on Skin*. I understand that the idea came from your daughter; is that correct?

Why did you feel it was necessary to change from the source, from troubadour to illuminator?

Pardon the curiosity, but why do you prefer that your work be described as "text for music" as opposed to "libretto"?

What are some of your extra-literary interests?

Mr. Crimp's answers:

Opera was never part of my cultural education and I came to my collaboration with George Benjamin as a playwright and theatre-practitioner. Therefore when I look at an opera, first and foremost I'm looking at a piece of theatre, and when I write a text for opera, I'm thinking about the creation of a coherent language-world, and the need to make strong transactions between characters -- just as I would in a play. The difference is, that I must leave out "the music" of my own (play) writing to provide the space for the true music of the composer. In practical terms a 90 minute play may be 70 pages long, while a 90 minute opera (composed syllabically) is about half that -- 35 pages of text. This means that within the text there's no room for what is not essential -- and the decision about what IS essential defines the taste of the writer-composer team. I would suggest that in the case of George and myself, what is essential is clear story-telling, coupled with emotional intensity. And these qualities have to be concentrated in the text so that they will blossom and grow with the music. I'm thinking about the paper flowers Proust describes -- tightly coiled paper structures that magically open up when placed in a jar of water.

Written on Skin is based on a 13th century razo -- a short anonymous biographical fantasy -- about the troubadour Guillem de Cabestanh. The idea of using a Provençal text came from Bernard Foccroulle, who commissioned the opera for the Festival d'Aix-en-Provence. At that time my daughter, who was studying modern and medieval French at Cambridge, and her supervisor Bill Burgwinkle, provided me with a Provençal reading-list. I was struck by the economy and clarity of the Coeur Mangé story -- and proposed it to George. A major adjustment was to turn the original troubadour into an illuminator of manuscripts (the 'Boy' in Written on Skin) principally to have access, in the writing, to a world of images via the descriptions of pictures.

You ask me what specific qualities I seek in a text for music* -- and I would say that in writing for George, I'm looking for images, because I know they inspire him. I don't think consciously of the 'sonority' of words -- but I am conscious of their rhythm -- and I'm quite meticulous about avoiding iambics, which can be deadly in contemporary English if over-used -- and I'm also sparing with Latinate words -- which means that "illumination", for example, becomes something of an event.

You also ask me what my extra-literary interests are. Well as it happens I'm interested in music -- more as an amateur pianist than as a concert-goer. One of the great pleasures of *Written on Skin* was to follow the process of composition, since George sent me the scenes as he wrote them. So as I muddled my way through the tricky chords and picked out the intertwined vocal lines -- clear lines sensitive to every nuance of human feeling -- I knew before anyone else -- except of course the composer -- that something remarkable was happening.

----

*I call it this (a) because I don't like the diminutive 'libretto', and (b) because as a stranger to opera I find this technical word alienating.

Chapter Three - Around the Opera

Some Trivia about Written on Skin

George Benjamin took two and a half years to compose the piece. During this period, according to him, he stopped conducting, teaching, traveling, and "almost stopped existing as a human being." He worked seven days a week, every week on the piece, and felt rather obsessed by it.

He felt that every single bar was impossible to write… until he did. After the conclusion he felt that the piece didn't belong to him any longer.

Benjamin thought that he had to make his opera feel natural, which is not easy in the 21st century as it was in the

19th century.

The composer invited the singers over to his house and played musical games with them to understand their vocal ranges and assets, in order to them write the vocal score.

He aimed at introducing the world of the troubadours through familiar sounds, but also unfamiliar ones, which is why he incorporated some rarely used instruments in his orchestration.

While not related to *Written on Skin,* a piece of interesting trivia regarding the composer's other opera, *Into the Little Hill,* is that when the piece had its country premiere at the Royal Opera House, the theater suffered an electric blackout which didn't include the bar. Patrons were invited to move to the bar and were given free drinks while electricians worked on the issue. After unsuccessful attempts to fix the problem, the chamber orchestra and the singers moved to the bar and presented the work there, sitting among the patrons.

Written on Skin has collected numerous sold-out performances around the world and has received consistent standing ovations at the end.

Martin's eldest daughter was studying French literature in Cambridge when she found the story and alerted her father and the composer to it.

Chapter Four - The Music of Written on Skin

Orchestration

Written on Skin is scored for a large orchestra. In terms of musical structure, the opera is through-composed (except that there are some brief thick silent pauses in some psychologically tense or pivotal moments), and uses a mix of tonal and atonal writing with poly-harmonic arrangements. Much tone painting is seen in various moments, such as the Angels getting hushed and ethereal sounds, heart beat being heard in double basses and plucked strings, anger building up on bass drums and exploding with fierce brass jabs, conflict seeping through vocal range leaps, and anxiety being expressed in halting, abrupt metric changes. Violence is underlined by crashing percussion with pebbles and bells. While there are no leitmotifs, some of the instruments acquire recurring themes, like the Protector's power finding its ways in the horns, and Agnès sensuality being brought up by the viola da gamba and orgasmic high harmonics in the violins.

The opera is orchestrated for three flutes (piccolo and alto), two oboes, two clarinets in Bb and A, a bass clarinet (Bb), a contrabass clarinet, two bassoons (one is a contrabassoon), four horns in F, four trumpets in Bb (one is a piccolo trumpet), three trombones, and a tuba, harp, glass harmonica, and bass viola da gamba.

The strings are in 8.6.6.6.4 player configuration. Two first violins double as mandolins, and all double basses must have extensions to low B natural.

The percussion section needs four players and is made of vibraphone, glockenspiel, three tubular bells, two crotales, five tuned cowbells, a low tenor steel drum, a low gong, a large tam-tam, two pairs of clash cymbals small and large, five suspended cymbals, two sets of sleighbells high and low, a small pair of claves, three mokubios, four temple blocks, three large pairs of maracas, guiro, whip, untuned cowbell, sandpaper blocks, a typewriter, two pairs of pebbles small and large, two small timpani, three mini-tablas (of which two are tuned very high), three high-pitched bongos, two side drums, two tenor drums, a tumba, and a bass drum.

As our readers can see, this is a large orchestra. However Benjamin rarely uses it all at once, and instead, adopts a minimalistic approach that often isolates a section of the orchestra. If by any chance you came to this chapter first, just trying to get informed about the music, do read George Benjamin's interview in an earlier chapter because he adds his own commentary to the musical devices he used (for example when he mentions omission and vacuum, and how some instruments only enter very late into the piece).

Vocal rhythms are intended to be close to natural speech patterns during free bars, and above all not strictly metrical. There are no ensembles. At times, there are brief duets and trios, but for the most part the voices either sing alone or overlap like people yelling at each other in a fight instead of having a true dialogue.

If we had to describe the music in Written on Skin in two words, the first one would have to be "colorful." George Benjamin was inspired by this medieval story about the writing of an illuminated book, and he paid attention to the bright palette of colors that these miniature paintings have. The second word must be "powerful." This music hits the listener like a brick, and is of rare intensity and density.

Scene-by-Scene Musical Commentary

The software used to compose this book does not have musical symbols so we had to use approximations.

PART ONE

I Chorus of Angels

The orchestra jumps immediately into a short burst marked "fast, energetic" from p to ff, followed immediately by the Angels chorus punctuated as they sing of "dismantling" cities of bricks by abrupt drums and brass hitting the aural scape like demolition balls. The word "strip" is extended and repeats a few times. The orchestra then quiets down to a hush as the countertenor starts singing from a pp marked "inaudible" into a poco a poco crescendo with a few beats from percussion instruments in the background. As Agnès and the Protector enter, we hear the orchestra again creating suspenseful sounds marked "strident" force. This alternates with the Angels describing the woman and the man in very slow, still tempi with calm pp dynamics.

II The Protector, Agnès and the Boy

The Protector sings in rather tonal lines over plucked strings contrasting with the legato in the voice, creating a sense of serenity and harmony while he describes his organized and methodical world – the calm before the storm that will shake his placid arrangements. As he asks for a book of illuminations, the high notes soar as if projecting his dream into space. As the boy shows the first illumination figures as an example of his art, the violins become melodious, with an eerie effect to underline the kind of beauty that is being demonstrated in the Boy's paintings. Colors abound in the pit and tempi accelerate slowly as other instruments join, to depict the Protector's growing enthusiasm with the Boy's art. Agnès, suspicious, starts singing in distressed, dissonant and jumpy high notes, countering her husband's desire, which angers him, producing in his singing wild metric oscillations in the same line (5/8, 2/4, 3/8, 2/4, 3/4 and back to 5/8) as he orders his wife: "His talent is clear. I'm satisfied. You will welcome him into our house" (See example 1, next page – all examples of vocal and piano score are authorized by Faber Music, for this book only).

The composer then engages in a goose-bumping transition with his triads falling apart into thick and ponderous dissonances that end scene II in a sustained run of low notes., to introduce a shift to the Angels who are about to make more comments – this is very impressive music, ripe with theatricality.

Example 1

III Chorus of Angels

Here we have the vocal lines behaving in striking contrast with the orchestra. The Angels comment upon the brutality and violence in Humankind's history therefore the vocal lines are fraught and bumpy while the orchestra seems to evoke the passage of time with much calmer writing.

IV Agnès and the Boy

Things get musically even more interesting in this scene. We see the first seduction attempts by Agnès and the realization of her sexuality, which is understated with pianissimi lines as if only whispering she might admit to these sinful feelings. Benjamin adopts a very creative way to depict this scene, using silence and barely audible sounds that seem like breathing. Benjamin stretches the tempo more and more as the Boy tells her she is too close, and she repeats "too close" a few times. Their voices start to overlap like people anxiously talking to each other, producing their own harmonies. Voice dynamics lower from pp to ppp, and the orchestra suddenly falls silent. This pivotal moment of silence when time seems to stop so that we know that huge transformations are about to come, leaks into vocal lines marked "hesitant" when Agnès proceeds to asking the boy to invent a more real woman in his drawings. At the end she sings "come to me" and the muted trumpet darkly matches her notes. It all, then, gets passionate and intense once Agnès is really made aware of what she is feeling when she literally shakes at the sight of the Boy like "light in a bowl splits and shakes on a garden wall" – Benjamin attacks this moment and the subsequent ones that follow, using six violins that overlap in muted and pizzicato patterns, with three second violins joining in tremolando, as well as contrabass clarinet, harp, and a flute. This is all done rather delicately from the orchestral restrained silent, in order to evoke a volcano of emotions slowly brewing into the characters, while we hear the tessitura of Agnès vocal line widening. Admirable tone painting! (Example 2).

Example 2

V The Protector and the visitors — John and Marie

As scene V sinks in, there is a brief interlude where the orchestra gets ominously loud again with abrupt flute and brass bursts marked "Strident" – this continues throughout this musically dissonant scene as it basically depicts the violence of the Protector, while he comments angrily on the changes he's been noticing in his wife, and while his sister-in-law Marie and her husband John question his unwise move of bringing a young boy into the household. As the scene ends, similarly strident sounds close it, like the ones heard at its beginning.

VI Agnès and the Boy

This scene is musically exquisite, and we hear the viol for the first time. Agnès is seen alone at the beginning of the scene, reflecting on what she wants, and her confusion and turmoil are demonstrated when she goes through a huge leap low-high-low in the word "wind" (see example 3a/b).

Example 3 a/b

When Agnès and the Boy get together in the scene and start to interact erotically, the vocal lines become very tuneful, delicate, pungent, and beautiful, with a flowing major third. Their love duet then grows slowly while a cello infuses it with intensity, and the viol adds melancholic notes with its peculiar sensual timbre – its sparse use in only a couple of scenes enhances the idea that the events rolling in are extraordinary and unusual. Medium and low brass get muted for a distant effect and add to the harmonic complexity, which is quite evident in the rather rich chords with up to ten notes written for the glass harmonica. As Agnès offers herself sexually to the Boy, we hear a quiet minor third in the glass harmonica, and we recover the sexual act itself in a thumping beat played by pizzicato double basses and the bass drum. The scene ends with Agnès producing the lowest note in all of her singing throughout the piece, when after she utters her own name in an affirmation of her powerful new identity achieved through her sexual liberation, she then lowers her voice more and more while she says "love is an act," and a heavy silence sinks in with the orchestra in ppp (see example 4).

Example 4

PART TWO

VII The Protector's bad dream.

The second part of the opera is where the orchestra and the vocal score become very tense, signifying the developing high tension of the drama and the troublesome events that will lead to the catastrophic conclusion in Part III. Accordingly, the score opens Part II with marks signaling "Very fast, nervous" and indeed so are the lines, while the orchestra engages in a continuous buzzing sound in the bass line with staccato, jumpy commentary in other instruments (example 5) and also in the halting voices: Angel 2 observes The Protector's damp skin while he dreams, and repeats the word "wet" six times ("wet like the white part of an egg") with Angel 3 observes "wet like a woman's mouth."

Example 5

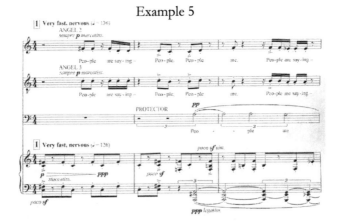

VIII The Protector and Agnès

As The Protector wakes up, his troubled thoughts are recovered in abrupt brass utterances, but when Agnès enters the scene the vocal score turns tender, calm, legatissimo, and she produces some very beautiful and delicate singing, showing her growing assurance paired with The Protector's discomfort. George Benjamin brings more instruments into this scene which contains a dense aural atmosphere. While Agnès becomes very sensual and eager, solo strings marked sul tasto and ppp signal her willingness for physical intimacy; when she is rebuffed by

The Protector, the pace accelerates and is marked fast and tense, however the instrumental music goes in the opposite direction, with muted brass and soft winds. This is a very interesting effect: instead of tone painting with the instruments, Benjamin makes the spectator sort of hold the breath and focus on the angry and frustrated woman's vocal lines, instead (example 6).

Example 6

As The Protector treats her like a child her notes soar up and leap into shrieks of anger, and she then reveals her affair with The Boy. The orchestra here explodes like a volcano. We get open ff brass and the winds run stronger and stronger and acquire rhythmic intensity. The writing for Agnès widens in range and goes to contemptuous low notes when she tells her husband with whom she is having the affair: "the one who writes on skin" (example 7a/b, next page).

While The Protector had staccato lines before while waking up from his dream, it is Agnès now who delivers her lines in aggressive punches. The orchestra becomes deafening until it abruptly stops, at scene end. Whew! Scene VIII is such a musical ride!

IX The Protector and the Boy

Scene IX is more serene in the orchestra (marked "subdued, though tense"), while The Protector and The Boy engage in a tentative vocal duel with flowing lines (especially for The Protector who has elongated, lamenting lines).

Example 7a/b

The tension and the danger are rendered rather by the percussion section, with several crashing sonorities. As The Protector gets more anxious while asking if it is with Agnès that the boy is sleeping, his singing resumes the halting staccato. Tension in the instruments drops immediately and serenity is recovered, once The Boy says that the name of his lover is Marie. The Protector goes confident again and sings with several metric changes, like in triumph.

X Agnès and the Boy

This is another nervous and loud scene especially in the vocal writing, with Agnès unleashing all her jealous fury.

The leaps are huge and go all the way to a twelfth, with the soprano at the end of the scene, with the full orchestra behind her producing intense volume, issuing a long top C on the word "blood," her highest note of the opera, which brings down the curtain on Part II (ex.8).

Example 8

PART THREE

XI The Protector, Agnès, and the Boy

The scene opens with tonal, melodic lines with plucked strings and winds. As The Boy describes his illuminations and links past and present, the percussion section comes alive, with many striking effects, including typing on a typewriter, low vibraphone (with extremely soft sticks) and suspended cymbals. All three principal singers participate in this scene, and the percussion conveys the underlying conflict.

XII The Protector and Agnès

While The Protector reads aloud the page of writing that describes his wife and The Boy making love, we get again the tense buzzing sounds in the orchestra, and the bursts of staccato utterances by the angry Protector. As the description gets more intensely erotic, the whole aural environment quiets and quiets, all the way down to pppp in The Protector's vocal line, in a very solemn moment (example 9).

Example 9

The tempo fastens and Agnès clearly reaches an orgasm, and moans repeatedly "ah... ah..." (Example 10), and she leaps up again, asking to see the word for Love in a high A. A brief and intense instrumental interlude brings up scene XIII.

Example 10

XIII Chorus of Angels and The Protector

This is one of the loudest scenes in the opera, filled to the brink with atonal and strident music, with no economy of means. Instruments play forte and purposefully mask and override the words in the vocal lines (like a horn solo obliterating the word "merciful" – a clever device, since there is no mercy in this scene, at all). Angel 2, Angel 3, and The Protector sing alternately loudly and softly – the alternation also gets to lines that are declamatory, versus others that are cantabile, to great dramatic effect. Benjamin then brings back his full orchestra to illustrate the Protector's violence and his murder of The Boy; all hell breaks loose. During the stabbing scene the violins get frenetic, and then once it is all done the brass section enters in full force, together with crashing percussion. The music is beautiful and powerful.

XIV The Protector, Agnès and the Angels

Here again, in this pivotal scene, we get loud jabs of brass punctuating the Protector's anger: "woman and her Protector" and boom! Then "night. A room" and boom again, all in fff (example 11). In one of the most literal illustrations in the work, the music is marked "keck" while Agnès is about to throw up, and the orchestra engages in clicking and popping sounds in the percussion (including pebbles) and sliding figures in the strings as she chews and swallows. Agnès' trouble is also recovered in fast metric changes as she comments on the food being sweet as her milk and salty as her tears.

Example 11

As The Protector reveals to her that she is eating the heart of her lover, his notes go into a sustained crescendo to its highest territory for him in the bass clef (example 12).

Example 12

She becomes defiant, and while she says that nothing he can do will ever take the taste of the Boy's heart from her mouth, look at the vocal leap from "Boy" to "heart", dear readers! (example 13), and here we go again to stratospheric territory in "mouth" with a seizure-inducing high C (example 14) while the 6-note chords that started the scene in those short trombone blasts and flurry of strings, now come to Agnès music – the composer definitely sides with her and transfer power from him to her, in a sensational musical illustration of this moment. Genius!

Example 13

Example 14

XV The Boy / Angel 1

The viol and the glass harmonica are back with the intended eerie effect, marked "floating, not slow." This is the musical moment when Katie Mitchell's brilliant staging incorporates slow motion in the choreographed displacements of Agnès and the angels through the rooms. The glass harmonica starts it all; a brief silence follows, and the viol takes over, while Angel 1 describes the woman falling. This is arguably the most musically beautiful moment in this opera (example 15a/b).

Example 15a

THE OPERA LIVELY GUIDES – WRITTEN ON SKIN

Example 15b

As The Boy keeps singing, the glass harmonica resumes and mixes with the viol and the voice; plucked strings are added, and his voice continues in a monologue that is eminently singable and even Italianate. As the tension increases and the climax of Agnès suicide approaches with all characters except the commenting Boy pursuing her upstairs in slow motion, there is a throbbing bass in D, a rustling of maracas, and clusters of strings going up to high C that is sustained and soft, like reproducing Agnès cry (example 16). It suddenly ends, as the final curtain falls. We are up for the inevitable standing ovation.

Example 16

Chapter Five - The Characters and their Voices

Let us talk about the characters in *Written on Skin*, and the notable performers who took upon themselves to do justice to this formidable work.

This chapter is best enjoyed by a reader with Internet access, since examples of singing mentioned here can be found on YouTube™ and the URL is included. At press time these URLs are current; however, there is no guarantee that these clips will remain up on YouTube™. The reader who is unable to find one of them (they are often removed by the uploaders or by YouTube™) should use the Search function of that website, to find similar examples. Including the URLs here is merely a service we are doing to our readers to facilitate their browsing of that trade-marked website, and in no way represents any endorsement of possible copyright violations by YouTube™ uploaders. The uploaders, not Opera Lively

Press, are responsible for those uploads and for verifying copyright.

There aren't at press time too many clips on YouTube™ of singers performing these role, but this one from the Royal Opera House does feature all three principal singers for a few seconds – Barbara Hannigan, Christopher Purves, and Bejun Mehta:

https://www.youtube.com/watch?v=onYj_-6yFw4

This ROH trailer contains a bit more:

https://www.youtube.com/watch?v=WsuTSOKYEF4

This ROH video clip contains the performers talking about their characters:

https://www.youtube.com/watch?v=8yUXhK7XmsI

This video from the Royal Swedish Opera features performances by singers Jeremy Carpenter, Elin Rombo, Bernhard Landauer, Susann Végh and Daniel Ralphsson:

https://www.youtube.com/watch?v=DExCtt9Ut2M

Let's talk briefly about each character.

Agnès

Agnès is a housewife, at first timid and subservient. It is unclear if her husband is already physically abusive to her as the opera opens, but certainly by the third part she has been beaten up and appears bruised. Agnès is intelligent and sensitive. She is sexually frustrated, asking her husband to kiss her, while being rebuffed with the judgmental statement that her behavior is childish. Her sexuality explodes when she encounters The Boy, and she becomes assertive, defiant, and eager for knowledge. Ultimately she kills herself as an act of affirmation, signaling to her husband that he won't have the pleasure of killing her because she will take her destiny on her own hands.

The role is the most difficult one in the opera, given that it requires a soprano capable of a wide range and of forceful, dramatic singing with brutal leaps, from solid low notes all the way to high C-sharps which occur in two scenes. Fortunately for the singer, it starts in the middle of the range for many bars, allowing her to warm up for the wild leaps that come next.

Canadian soprano Barbara Hannigan created the role and repeated it numerous times. Other sopranos who have sung or are scheduled to sing the role include Elin Rombo, Miriam Clark, Vera-Lotte Böcker, Evellyn Pollock, and Lauren Snouffer.

The Protector

The Protector is Agnès husband. He is cruel, orders killings in his lands to keep his subjects subdued, and believes that his wife is his property. He is grandiose and commissions a book to celebrate the greatness of his family. In a jealous fit he kills his wife's lover and attempts to kill her too. In terms of tessitura, this role for bass-baritone is not very demanding as it doesn't go too high or too low. The main issue for the singer resides in frequent metric changes and the need for a lot of color, since The Protector's state of mind changes constantly. British bass-baritone Christopher Purves created the role and performed it in most runs given by the major houses. He defines the various colors like this: "I try to weep with the voice, to curse, to threaten, to exult, to tear, to rip, to cut, to cajole, to plead, to love." There is even a bit of grunting. Other singers who tackled the role in smaller houses include Evez Abdulla, Andreas Jören, Jordan Shanahan, Jeremy Carpenter, Audun Iversen, and Evan Hughes.

The Boy

The Boy is an artist who paints illuminations on parchment. He is hired by The Protector to create a book celebrating his family and his exploits. He is sensitive and poetic, and his colorful paintings and clever wording introduce a new element of eroticism in The Protector's household. He has an affair with the wife and is murdered by the husband. The singer in this role also doubles as Angel 1, commenting upon the events. It is a countertenor role. Again, the tessitura is not much of a problem as it sits on the usual countertenor range, predominantly middle and low regions of the range. Much of it is declamatory, with good space given to the singer by the orchestration. American countertenor Bejun Mehta created the role in Aix-en-Provence and repeated it at the Royal Opera House. Other singers who performed the role include Tim Mead, Terry Wey, Bernhard Landauer, Iestyn Davies, and Augustine Mercante.

The Two Comprimario Roles

Angel 2 / Marie is Agnès sister. She appears briefly, criticizing her brother in law for introducing The Boy into the household. She also appears in a scene in which as The Boy falsely reports to The Protector that he is sleeping with her instead of Agnès, the imaginary affair is depicted. She also doubles as Angel 2, commenting on the action. It is a role for a mezzo-soprano. This role is difficult not in terms of range, but rhythmically it has many metric changes and requires many leaps between the chest voice and the head voice. Also, it is not accompanied very steadily by instruments so the singer needs to have a clear notion of the pitch. It was created by American mezzo Rebecca Jo Loeb in Aix-en-Provence, then performed by Victoria Simmonds at the Royal Opera House. Other singers in this role have included Tammy Coil, Susanne Blattert, Anna Werle, Theresa Holzhauser, and Susan Végh.

Angel 3 / John is a small tenor role, for Marie's husband who sings a few lines in one scene, and comments briefly on the action. It doesn't encompass major difficulties. The role was created by British tenor Allan Clayton in Aix-en-Provence, and he repeated it in London and Paris. Other singers have included Tamás Tarjányi, Markus Gruber, Nik Kevin Koch, Daniel Ralphsson, and Isaiah Bell.

Chapter Six - Discography

Recordings in Audio and Video and Vocal Score

As of this guide's press time, there is one recording in audio, and two in video of *Written on Skin*. The most recent video recording is from the Royal Opera House. A very similar video circulated temporarily on the Internet as pay-per-view from Medici TV, recorded live at Aix-en-Provence. It is very similar to the ROH Blu-ray with the same staging and scenery and the same cast of principal singers. Now that the ROH has released their high-quality 1080p, DTS-HD 5.1 recording, the previous Medici TV file is only of historical importance therefore we won't comment upon it. In the next pages we'll mostly address the Blu-ray. It should be also noted that the vocal score is available in print from Faber Music on paperback, sold in Great Britain for about 28 GBP and in the American market for about $36, with ISBN 10: 0571526721, and ISBN 13: 978-0571526727.

Audio (CD)

The opera has been released on CD. Sound quality is not the most ideal in this live recording from the premiere in Aix-en-Provence (July 7, 2012), but is adequate. Given that the same principal singers figure in the Blu-ray Disc version and frankly their performances in these two products are rather similar, we will comment on their artistry in the next part. As of press time, the going rate for this CD in the American market was about $16. In Great Britain the going price is about 12 GBP.

It includes a short work (Duet) for piano and orchestra in disc 2, featuring pianist Pierre Laurent Aimard.

Nimbus Records, 2 CDs, released on July 9, 2013, ASIN B009VECK8Q – Catalog number NI 5885/6 – Playing time 90' 38" - Mahler Chamber Orchestra conducted by George Benjamin – Recording of the first performance, world premiere, Festival d'Aix en Provence, July 2012. Barbara Hannigan is Agnès, Bejun Mehta is The Boy and Angel 1, Christopher Purves is The Protector, Rebecca Jo Loeb is Marie and Angel 2, Allan Clayton is John and Angel 3.

The two booklets include an interview with Benjamin, illustrated bios of the performers, background and the full text, with a synopsis.

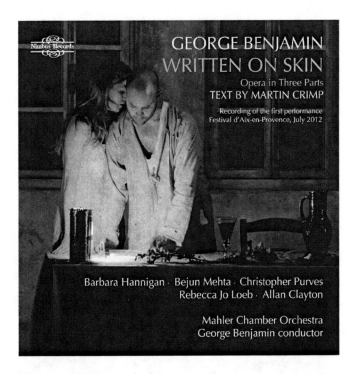

Video (DVD, Blu-ray disc)

There are both DVD and Blu-ray Disc versions of the same video recording of this opera. As of press time, the going rate for these items in the American market were approximately $27 for the DVD and $36 for the Blu-ray Disc (list price $39.99). In the British market, the DVD was going for about 23 GBP, and the Blu-ray for 24 GBP.

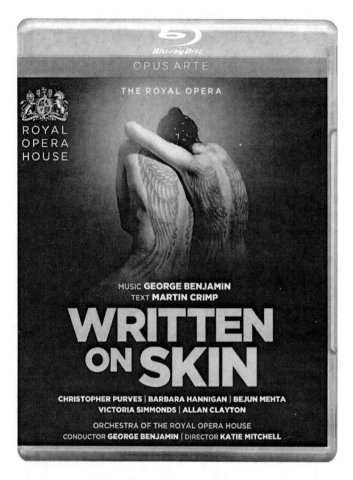

The Daily Telegraph deemed this product "Music of genius... superb performances from a flawless cast."

This Opus Arte recording was released on January 12, 2014, with ASIN B00GJ6KCSO and catalog number OA BD7136 D. It is sung in English and contains subtitles in English, French, German, and Japanese. Runtime is 90 minutes for the opera with 8 minutes of bonus. Audio formats are LPCM 2.0 and DTS-HD Master Audio 5.1.

Image format is aspect ratio 16:9, filmed in high definition 1080p. All regions.

This is a Royal Opera House production, produced and directed for the screen by Margaret Williams. It features the Orchestra of the Royal Opera House conducted by George Benjamin. Stage director is Katie Mitchell, Designs are by Vicki Mortimer, and Lighting by Jon Clark. The cast is the same of the CD above, except for Marie/Angel 2, sung by Victoria Simmonds. The insert contains a 4-page essay by Christopher Wintle and the official synopsis written by Martin Crimp himself (the same one we reproduced here in this book). These pages are repeated in French and German. There are four color production pictures, one of them large (over two central pages) showing most of the stage. The performance on this disc was recorded live at the Royal Opera House, Covent Garden, London, in March of 2013.

The bonus contains eight minutes of presentation by Pappano, with words from George Benjamin, Martin Crimp, the stage director and the three principal singers. It's short but compelling. Then there is a slightly longer interview with the composer.

Acting is of the highest possible quality by all involved. Barbara Hannigan's voice is amazingly strong and precise in all registers and she seems to navigate the leaps at ease. Bejun Mehta is delicate and pure in tone, and his intense gaze adds a formidable dimension to the scenes. Chris Purves couldn't depict the troubled Protector any better. Video direction is very interesting with some takes from the roof. Sets are lighting are beautiful and stage direction is of rare talent with rather perfect blocking, including the genial touch of slow motion in the last scene. This is an A++ product all the way.

Chapter Seven - Singing and Acting in Written on Skin

Interviews with Performers

Barbara Hannigan

Canadian soprano Barbara Hannigan is just amazing. She conducts, dances, plays the piano, and sings, and champions modern and contemporary music like nobody. She is also a phenomenal actress, and talking to this multi-talented woman in July 2013 was a pleasure. We called her on the phone from Santa Fe; she was relaxing at home in Canada.

Luiz Gazzola for Opera Lively - Thank you Ms. Hannigan, for doing this. I'm very impressed with your Agnès in *Written on Skin.* You are a wonderful artist, so it will be my honor and my pleasure to interview you, having talked at length with the composer George Benjamin about this piece – he is obviously another great admirer of your talent. Let's start by talking about your character. It's a very emotionally intense character, one that must resonate with a performer's inner core. Please talk to us about the psychology of the character.

Barbara Hannigan – The psychology of Agnès? Obviously the role is about liberation. As far as she is concerned, she is dealing with a situation in which she didn't know how oppressed she was. The way that I play her is that from the beginning it is clear that she is frustrated, but she doesn't really understand why; she doesn't know what she is missing. As the opera goes on, this boy comes into the house, and he evokes feelings in her that are confusing and very strong. He encourages her to think and feel. Then the trajectory of events is quite intense.

OL - What exactly triggers Agnès sudden defiance of her abusive husband?

BH – Nothing is a sudden choice for her. Every step that she makes is one small step, and that is made very clear in the libretto at the beginning. She is remembering how she took her shoes off and that she wouldn't make a lot of sound, and she quietly walks up the steps to the boy's room for the first time, to see what he was painting. She walks over to him in very tiny little steps. I don't think she talks to herself "I am going to have an affair with him and change my life." It's really more "I'm curious, I have these feelings inside and I don't know what they are, so for the first time in my life I'm really going to follow my heart and my instinct."

OL – Yes, very interesting! You are right, now that I think of it – it is indeed gradual, not sudden. Why do you think Agnès kills herself? Would it be a matter of control, to rob her husband of the opportunity to murder her?

BH – You are right, that's part of it. It's her final act of power, certainly. It's a very powerful and defiant act for her to do that. At that time suicide was the ultimate sin. It's also a liberating choice, because if she stays, either he will kill her, or will make of her life a living hell, so her only escape, really, is to jump off the window. She has liberated herself intellectually, sexually, emotionally, and has begun to be her own person. She is no longer owned by her husband, and so this is her final act of ownership: "I decide how I die, and when I die."

OL - *Written on Skin* has scenes that are of a devastating eroticism, but done in a classy way by stage director Ms. Katie Mitchell without showing any… skin.

BH – Right!

OL - I personally see it as a lesson to be learned by certain Regie directors. What are your views on the issue of Regieoper?

BH – It's an interesting question. I see that term used and I often have the feeling that it is used in a negative way, against directors who don't respect the real story of an opera. They will take an opera and turn the story upside down, and make of it something very different than what the singers are singing about, and everyone needs to twist themselves upside down and backwards to try and make it work. But my feeling is that I do think opera needs very good directors. It's no longer a performance of standing and singing, and pretty costumes and pretty sets. The public also wants to have good actors and good direction even when they are seeing traditional opera like bel canto or Mozart or Handel, as well as with contemporary works like *Written on Skin*.

I just want to work with a team that clicks, when you have a director who respects the story and the characters, and who has an understanding of the music to the best of their ability. Then, we have a conductor and a music staff who are also supporting this Gesamtkunstwerk. Then, we have a very special situation. If I look at two operas I did this year, *Written on Skin* and *Lulu*, that's what we got. In *Written on Skin*, there was Katie's beautiful and intense direction. She kept talking to us about how she didn't want our gestures to be "operatic." She didn't want to go to Opera Land. She wanted it to be real and feel more like theater, or even more filmic. She was constantly telling us to do less.

With *Lulu* directed by Krysztof Warlikowski, there was hesitation in the opera world about his work, which I cannot understand, because he is absolutely an extraordinary colleague and director. He worked very much from the center of the story of *Lulu*. When I walked into the very first rehearsal and we began to speak, I thought "We have exactly the same ideas about this woman." All the crazy things I did in *Lulu*, going on pointe [ballet shoes], falling down, time and time again being pushed around the stage, any of the extreme physical things I did in that piece, certainly fit what was happening both in the libretto and the music. It all made perfect sense.

We really need this compatible marriage between the director, the conductor, and of course, singers who are interested and willing to do more than just stand and sing, to really incorporate – in the true sense of the word – the characters.

OL - How do you feel about the smashing success of *Written on Skin*? Did you expect this much ever since you laid eyes on the piece?

BH – I didn't. First of all, I often don't think about whether something is a hit or not. But certainly, when I get a new score, I think "Is this a good score?" I make my decisions very quickly. Sometimes my perspective changes over the period of rehearsal, but quite early on in the process I have an opinion, shall we say. [Laughs] But I didn't have any idea that this would be such a success. As we were working with Katie during the rehearsal process, it became clear that this was something very special. We started to really love the piece and the process of working on it. As we got to the dress rehearsal in Aix-en-Provence, people had been coming to the rehearsals and there was a lot of buzz about the piece.

We were in the biggest theater in Aix-en-Provence, and it was a risk to put modern opera in this theater where the Berlin Philharmonic had done the *Ring*. The response was extraordinary for opening night, but then there were no tickets to be had – it was just completely sold out. This was a wonderful feeling and a wonderful surprise. Except perhaps for Amsterdam – I wasn't there, I was singing *Lulu* at the time so I couldn't be part of that – every other location we've gone to, the opera has been sold out. Even in Munich, I've never seen an audience respond like that. The curtain calls just went on, and on, and on.

The opera appeals to the heart of the public. They become wrapped up in the story as if it were a kind of thriller. I don't think they sit there saying "Oh, I'm enjoying modern opera." They don't seem to think of it as modern opera. They are so engrossed in the story, because it is transfixing. Then they go home and tell their friends, and they read about it, and everyone comes. I haven't heard any negative words. No one has come up to me and said "Oh, what a waste of time." It's been the opposite.

OL - I know you're no stranger to creating new operatic roles and I'll ask about it a little later, but right now, to remain on the *Written on Skin* topic, let me ask you this: The experiencing of creating a role for a piece that is being heralded as the best masterpiece of the 21st century so far, and one that is in all likelihood destined to withstand the test of time, must be thrilling. Any comments on this particular effect of – let's call it this way, immortality - that this is likely to have in your legacy as a singer?

BH – First and foremost, it's a great honor and it is very good fortune to be part of this. It's a combination of a long commitment that I had to music – to singing it and performing it, and particularly, modern music. I've premiered over 80 works, and I know every one of them won't be a hit or a masterpiece. I didn't know what I was getting into with George's opera because I hadn't seen a single note of the score when I said "Yes, I will do it." I didn't even know the story.

When we look at the history books and look at the singers for whom particular roles were written – like Mary Garden who premiered Mélisande, or we remember Maria Malibran or Adelina Patti – all these singers were modern music singers. I'm really excited that my name gets in some way to be beside those names. It's a great, great honor.

OL - How did George Benjamin pick you?

BH – I don't know! I've known George for quite some time, and he certainly knows my work. We have many, many colleagues in common. He's seen me perform. All I know is that he came up to me in Luzern quite some years ago and just flat out asked me if I would be in his opera, and once we sorted out the times and so on, that was really it. He had an idea when he asked me. He knew the character of the piece that I would sing – I didn't. He very much wrote the part for me, so he had the upper hand. He knew what he wanted and what he was doing – I was a bit in the dark. I had to discover the part scene by scene.

I think every composer that I work with projects something of themselves on to me, or on to any of the people for whom they are writing. In George's case, as you know, Agnès is a very heart-breaking character. She garners a lot of sympathy from the audience. I was thinking yesterday – if he changed the story a bit, it didn't have to be a woman, it's not particularly that; it's just one of these persons who need to free themselves. Everyone has the opportunity to go through that at some point in their lives, in a small way or a large way.

OL - Can you please share with us memories of the composition process, and how George got input from the singers? I know that George invited you all over to talk about the tessitura.

BH – He already knew my voice and my repertoire. He looked at the pieces I've sung and knew what my voice can do. That said, I went to his house and we very carefully played a kind of compositional game together, where he would write a few notes and then ask me to write on the music paper what kinds of notes I wanted to come next, then he'd write a few more notes and I'd write a few more notes. By this game, he started to see how my voice likes to move. One of the things he saw is that I love to make very large leaps from low to high or from high to low. If you look at the role of Agnès, that's what happens. She starts with very small intervals in the opening scenes, and then as she becomes liberated the intervals become larger and larger until the final aria which has a range of an octave and a fifth. She is constantly leaping more than an octave in her most fantastic final aria just before she kills herself. George really listened to me, which I loved.

OL – Isn't it incredible, how he manipulates the music to fit the situation? This opera is so brilliant! I think it is one of the top three contemporary operas I've ever seen, and I go as far as ranking it in the top twenty of all time. People gave me flack about it, but I stand by it. I think it is one of the top twenty operas ever composed.

BH – Yes, I think you are right.

OL - How hard is the Agnès role as a sing, as a vocal challenge, even though it was written for your voice?

BH – It's hard to sing, yes. It is difficult. But it has a natural progression of the role, so as the energy builds up, it gives me the energy to sing. As the character becomes more and more energetic I'm also energetic, and as she starts to break out then I need to break out at the same time. As long as I do a good warm up… and when I start to sing the piece in performance, it also warms me up, vocally. It doesn't start with spectacular high notes, or spectacular pianissimo. It's very controlled in a middle voice way, then it spirals and becomes bigger and bigger and bigger. So actually this makes it easier to sing, at least for me.

OL - Those who have seen the world premiere and the Covent Garden run have by now associated the three main roles with the role creators, you, and your wonderful colleges Mr. Mehta and Mr. Purves. How is for you, the work with other casts now that the opera is being revived everywhere? I asked George and he said he did not have to adapt the vocal score to other singers, so far.

BH – It was quite early on that Bejun Mehta had to be replaced. We had a wonderful guy in Toulouse named Tim Mead. He brought something very different to the role, he brought a kind of tenderness and compassion which was really sweet to experience, and he sang beautifully. I really enjoyed it. And then we had another countertenor in Vienna and Munich, Iestyn Davies, who had worked with Katie Mitchell before, so he particularly understood her appreciation for a certain kind of acting. I also enjoyed working with him. Vocally, everyone is different, and Bejun has some incredible strengths, especially in the lower register which is very difficult for countertenors, so sometimes I miss that particular beauty of tone, but everyone has their strengths, and all three countertenors that have sung the part have bought something to it.

Only once we had a different person to replace Christopher Purves, only in Vienna, and it was a Norwegian singer named Audun Iversen, and I thought he did a very good job, but there wasn't as much...[she hesitates] Because Bejun had to be replaced several times, I'm used to working with different countertenors, but with the new Protector we only had a few performances, and it is more difficult to connect if you know you are only going to do it once. I think he did a beautiful job. He was younger and he was a really big guy – I mean, a lot younger than Chris. The thing about playing it with Chris is that I was the young wife, whereas with Audun we were more or less the same age and it leveled out the playing field a little bit. When I'm the oppressed wife with the much older husband – Chris Purves is not that much older than me, but on stage he looks older and I look younger – it's a different dynamic.

OL - You've just finished another sold out run of this spectacular opera in Munich, and I know about the Paris run later this year. Do you have plans to revive the role, and if yes, where and when, if you are at a liberty to say it?

BH – Yes, there are plans to do it in New York in 2015. It will be fully staged; not in an opera company, but part of a festival. I'm not authorized to be more specific. There are plans for us to return to Covent Garden for it, and we will also do it in concert form in Toronto, and there are other offers coming in as well. There is a ton of interest. It's a pity that I won't be able to do them all.

OL - Not only you have incorporated into your repertoire this gorgeous role of Agnès, but you risk to become a quite iconic Lulu as well. Can you tell us about the impact of playing and singing Lulu?

BH – Ah, it was amazing. It was really one of those "the role of your lifetime." It's such a huge part; to prepare it is more than one year of work, not just vocally but also emotionally, in the attempts to incorporate such an extraordinary character. I felt really fortunate that we had Krysztof Warlikowski as our director, because he and I worked very much of one mind. I'm happy that he and I have other projects together in the future. We have two more operas that we will do together. It was very hard for me to let go of Lulu when I finished the nine performances in Brussels. It had been sold out and incredibly well received by almost all the press. It was very hard to say goodbye to this vision. I have the feeling that I didn't really say goodbye. I think Lulu became part of everything else I do. What she taught me as a character has infused other roles and even other concerts I did ever since, including Agnès.

OL – Interesting. Now, let's shift to other aspects of your illustrious career. First of all, I'd like to ask you why a Canadian-born artist has been so prolific in Europe but hasn't been back to perform in your native North America as often – maybe just a question of opportunity, but if there are specifics about this choice I'd like to hear about them, if you don't mind. We miss you here, Ms. Hannigan. Any plans to sing and conduct more often this side of the Atlantic?

BH – I am asked for lots of things in North America. I'm really particular about what I do, and often times it's just a matter of the calendar, with something not fitting. I do come to Canada every couple of years to sing with the Toronto Symphony Orchestra and I have a wonderful relationship with them. I do have plans in the major cities in the United States over the next couple of years to do various programs. I'm really happy with those relationships. I think you'll see once the seasons are announced for 2015 and 2016 that I'm over in the States a fair bit doing some really wonderful repertoire and also bringing some special pieces that I created in Europe to the United States. So, I'm really looking forward to that.

OL - Then, we can't help but being amazed at your artistry combining singing, conducting, dancing, and playing the piano. Would you tell us how this multi-talented career came to be like this? How do these passions have intertwined with each other in your training? What fulfills you more as an artist – singing recitals and concerts, singing opera, accompanying yourself on the piano, dancing, or conducting? Of course, most probably, all of the above, but still, there must be some difference in your enjoyment of these different aspects of your art.

BH – Well, the singing is of course the central guiding force, and I think everything else is an extension of that. I always played piano, and occasionally I will play accompanying myself in public, but only for special projects. I am not going to go play a concerto somewhere or anything like that. It's more having a kind of theatrical aspect to it when I sit down and accompany myself.

The conducting is also an extension of the leadership I have when I sing. Certainly I try to be the best musician that I can be, so I've always had a strong awareness of what my colleagues are doing in the orchestra. When it was suggested to me that I tried to conduct as well – actually it wasn't even my idea – I became quite addicted to that way of studying a score and that kind of preparation. It is really very addictive to prepare a score with that depth. I don't have as much time as I would like when I'm "just the singer" but when I have to prepare a score for conducting it does take a lot of time and a lot of attention, but it's the kind of work that I absolutely thrive on.

As far as the dancing goes, I have had dance training as a younger person and I have done a lot of modern dance pieces in which I also had to sing, over the years, but it became a much more prevalent part of my work since 2010 when I started working with Sasha Waltz, the choreographer in Berlin.

I had always been quite a physical performer and I've always been in a strong physical condition, but when it started with Sasha, it was eight hours a day of dancing and training, and I was singing as well, and was expected to be one of the dancers. I was intimidated by it at first, but I also felt in a way quite liberated and very excited, because I was doing something that I have always dreamed of. I always wanted to dance, but I had to choose music because where I came from in Nova Scotia you couldn't do everything, otherwise you would spend your entire life in the car, driving from lesson to lesson. It would have been impossible; then I chose to focus on music, and it is fantastic that later on in my life I actually get to live another dream.

OL – Did you take conducting lessons, or was it self-taught?

BH – When I began conducting, when I made my debut, to be honest I actually hadn't had more than a few hours of coaching. It came quite naturally, but I didn't have a disciplined technique. I just did it. Maybe it was just like the dancing. I had some lessons as a young person but I actually just went out there and did it. Now I am taking lessons. When I prepare a score, I work with Jorma Panula in Finland who is the conducting guru, a fantastic teacher. So now when I prepare a score I go to Helsinki and I work with him. It gives me more confidence and confirms a lot of the instincts I have. He is not showing me how to conduct. He is helping the conducting emerge out of me as a musician. He doesn't say "move your arms like this or like that." He is really drawing out the most efficient and most musical way of showing the orchestra what I want. That's what I really needed; I think it's what every conductor needs.

OL - You have sung with some of the best conductors of today. Does your work as a conductor yourself, informs your interaction with them? Do you have a better say than other singers when you work with conductors?

BH – Yes, I think that's true. It works the other way around too. I always respect all my colleagues, but now I do see the score in a different way. I know how difficult it is to conduct, and when I'm working with conductors, it probably makes the working together a little bit easier because I know what they are trying to show me or what they need from me, and I realize more clearly what I need from them. There are just so many things going on that they need to control or be aware of in the orchestra! So I guess I have more empathy for what they are doing. I get to work with such amazing colleagues; players and conductors. Sometimes I'm pinching myself and thinking "How did this all happen?"

OL - You are very devoted to Baroque and to modern and contemporary music, a somewhat unusual combination. Would you tell us what attracts you in these very different approaches to music; one so tonal and melodious, one so fragmented? (By the way, I must say, I also love both).

BH – It's something about the purity of the sound creation that I really like about the Baroque and classical music. There is something really clean about it, about the tuning and the architecture of the score, and I could see that comparison as well in the modern repertoire. It is why often in the singing it works very well side by side, having those two styles of music as my focuses.

OL - What do you think we need to do to expose more the traditional operatic audiences to all the extraordinarily good work being done today by some of our contemporary operatic composers? The audiences sometimes are spoiled with the romantic pieces and don't accept as well the dissonance and atonality of the modern pieces.

BH – One of the most important things is the way programs are made. If we put an entirely contemporary music program on a season, it's very hard for the audience. It's like looking at four very difficult pieces of modern art side by side – it's exhausting. I like to have programs that are mixed but have a true line, of course, of some connection between the pieces, but they are also like a journey where you have moments that are very intense and drain a lot from the emotional side, from the intellect, and other moments which are slightly more restful and allow us to have some piece for a while. It's like a landscape. Those people who are making programs – sometimes now that is me, because I'm doing a lot of programming as well – need to consider the stamina of the audience. We want to challenge them, and we want to appeal to them especially in an emotional way as opposed to an intellectual way. How can we draw them in to the dramatic component of the evening? It's the most important thing.

I don't like all kinds of contemporary music. I'm very, very picky about who I promote and what music I sing. I'm very careful, because I know that when I sing a particular contemporary piece, I am telling everyone "This is what I want you to listen to." So, I need to be very, very strict; and I am, about what I will agree to sing.

OL - We on Opera Lively make a point of covering new works as much as we can – I'm here in Santa Fe for the world premiere of *Oscar*. So, like I said you are a very frequent role creator. Besides Agnès, you have taken part in the world premières of Pascal Dusapin's *Passion* (Lei) at the Aix Festival, Louis Andriessen's *Writing to Vermeer* (Saskia) for the Netherlands Opera, Jan van de Putte's *Wet Snow* (Liza) for the Nationale Reisopera of the Netherlands, Michel van der Aa's solo opera *One* with film and electronics, Luca Mosca's *Signor Goldoni* (Despina) at La Fenice and Gerald Barry's *The Bitter Tears of Petra von Kant* (Gabrielle) for the English National Opera. I don't mean to ask you about all of them because it would be too lengthy, but would you please pick some that you care about the most, describe them briefly to us, and share with us some of the experience of singing these characters?

BH – *Passion* by Dusapin is a major work in my repertoire, I would say. I performed it in three different stagings. We had three different directors for this piece. It was written for me. Well, all of those pieces were written for me. I loved that I was able to explore the character in three different ways, and continue to do so, because we still have performances of that opera in the future. It's a very special piece for me.

Gerald Barry is really a composer I admire greatly. He is a friend, and he is an artist whom I honor very much. *The Bitter Tears of Petra von Kant* was the first opera of his that I did, then he wrote a Strindberg play called *La Plus Forte – The Stronger* – into an opera, for me, for one soprano and orchestra, and I've been performing that for several years, although we've never done it staged; we've only done it in concert. He also wrote *The Importance of Being Ernest*, and the role of Cecily was written for me. And now he is writing an opera on *Alice in Wonderland* and I will be Alice. So, he is a very important colleague in my life, and he is an incredible creative force. One of the things about him that is so special is that he's got a fantastic sense of humor in his music, because music doesn't generally tend to be very funny. Ligeti can make things funny, but there are not very many other composers who can do that, and Gerald Barry is one of them.

OL - Please tell us about the *Let me tell you*, for soprano and orchestra you'll be singing soon and in 2014.

BH – It's a half an hour piece, by Hans Abrahamsen who is a Danish composer, and Paul Griffiths who is a Welsh writer. It's a very special piece. I've just gotten the score for it, actually, and I'm so excited, because the premiere is in December with the Berlin Philharmonic, and it came out of a book that Paul Griffiths wrote about Ophelia, from Shakespeare. To make a long story short, I basically asked the Berlin Philharmonic to commission Hans Abrahamsen to write a piece for me and the orchestra using text from this book. What I find amazing about it is that before the score was even written, we already had many orchestras that were interested to have me come and sing it, including the Göteborgs Symfoniker, the

Rotterdam Philharmonic with Yannick Nézet-Séguin, and we will sing it at the Concertgebouw; we will sing it in Birmingham; so it's an amazing project, and it is a very special piece. You will be able to watch it in December in the Digital Concert Hall in Berlin; they will broadcast it online. What I love is that it came from the artists; it didn't come from a manager trying to put famous people together. It came from me, Paul, and Hans, just from the artistic idea we brought, and tried to bring it as we have done, to the highest level. To have the Berlin Philharmonic premiere it is just extraordinary; we still can't really believe it.

OL - Your impressive discography boasts 13 items already that I could count (maybe more that I haven't noticed), between DVDs and CDs. Do you have favorites? Would you describe to us a couple of very special CD items for you, and how you got to select the music for them?

BH – I don't know, because I never listen to them. First of all, it's a Dutilleux recording, *Correspondances*, that's probably the most important to me. It's a piece that I sung for almost ten years and I worked very, very much with that composer, and with Esa-Pekka Salonen and the Orchestra of Radio France. We made this beautiful recording which has been very, very well received. I would say that people should listen to that piece, definitely.

The other CD of course that just came out was *Written on Skin*.

Again, I can't say that I actually listen to them. I make the recording, but I don't listen to it once it is out, although I have it. [Laughs] I remember those days when we recorded Written on Skin; they were live performances in Aix-en-Provence, and I know the feeling, and I know that the recording is a very good representation of those incredibly exciting moments around those first performances of what you have said is a masterpiece.

And the third recording that I like a lot is *Les Illuminations*, by Benjamin Britten, which I recorded with the Amsterdam Sinfonietta. I'm very happy with it; I think it's a very good piece, and I'm happy that I was able to record it with that group.

OL - Let's end if you don't mind by a couple of questions about the person underneath the artist. Please tell us how was for you, growing up with this passion for classical music.

BH – I come from a very small village in Nova Scotia. When I was growing up there wasn't any Internet. We didn't have a public transportation system, so we couldn't go out to attend a concert or something like that in an easy way. We could get in a car and drive one hour or two hours, but we did a lot of music in the home. The school music program was very important, because we had very, very good music teachers. The kids, my friends at school, everybody was excited about music and music-making. It certainly wasn't anything sophisticated that we did, but I really loved making music for as long as I can remember. It really was love. It wasn't that I liked it, it was that I loved it. When I moved to the big city, to Toronto, all of a sudden I could go to the Symphony five nights a week. I could hear chamber music programs, and I could spend several hours in the library listening to recordings and scores, and that was like a festival for me, because I was so hungry and so curious!

OL – How old were you when you moved to Toronto?

BH – I was seventeen.

OL – Was your family involved in music as well? Were your parents musicians?

BH – My parents were involved in music in an amateur way, nothing professional. But my sister studied cello, and she is a professional cellist. She lives in Montreal. She had really seriously good training with Yehudi Menuhin who took her when she was fifteen to a summer program in Spain and in Switzerland. She was a very high level musician. My twin brother did his degree in music. He focused on jazz, but he didn't stay in the business; he decided to go into something else. Three out of the four kids really studied very intensely. We all played the piano, plus another instrument, plus singing lessons, choir camp; a lot of music all the time.

OL - Please tell us about your extra-musical interests. What else do you enjoy and love, in your life outside of the performing universe?

BH – The thing I like to do most other than making music is to cook. I love it. I tend to make really elaborate meals and to create recipes. I can't follow a recipe. It's not in my nature. I will read books and cooking magazines, whatever, but I always have to make up my own path, which is probably like my music career as well, [laughs] I certainly don't follow a recipe in my music career. That's one of my main hobbies. The other thing is that I can't say I'm very good at relaxing, because I like to work, and I like to work hard, but when I'm home like I am now, I can sit and read a book, and I can visit with my family, and I can enjoy the beautiful nature that we have in Canada, and that's very important to me, to reconnect in a very basic way with my surroundings.

OL – Do you have any causes that you plan to be active in, like education of children, or something like that?

BH – As far as teaching goes, I do like to give workshops for composers and master classes for singers. I like working with kids, but I find it exhausting. I think every teacher knows what I am talking about. [Laughs] It's really exhausting. It gives you a lot of energy but it also takes a lot of energy from you, and right now what I'm expanding into, in the conducting, is taking pretty much all of my time. So, I don't see myself doing a major educational program and spending a few weeks of every year teaching.

OL - I know that this question is always a bit of a challenge but it is very nice for our readers to get a flavor of the person: how do you define your personality? How are you, as a person?

BH – I'm pretty high energy. [Laughs] I have a lot of energy. I'm very positive. I have literally trained my mind to be very positive in the way I approach everything that I do, kind of like sports psychology, so that I can be as healthy as I can. I suppose I'm quite driven. I like to work hard; I like to keep a very fast pace. It's hard for me to sit still. It's hard for me to relax. For me, relaxing is studying, or making programs for a festival, so this is a little bit funny. I think I'm a pretty happy and positive person. I have down times when I feel frustrated and less positive, especially when I'm tired or things are going wrong. I like to have schedules of what I'm doing. For some reason if something goes wrong I don't have a lot of room to adjust. Certainly my colleagues usually say that I'm pretty positive and fun to work with and pretty intense. [Laughs].

OL – One can tell, looking at your schedule. [Laughs] I'm grateful for this interview, you answered our questions so well and for so long! I'll be thrilled to see you in New York in 2015, or maybe sooner. I was about to travel to Paris to go see *Written on Skin* there, but it coincides with my son's college graduation.

BH – Oh, I see, you can't miss that. Well, I'm glad that we talked, and that we had the time to answer all the questions. Thank you so much!

This interview is also feature online on Operalively.com with complete artistic biography, discography, pictures, and video clips. Type the following URL on your browser:

http://operalively.com/forums/content.php/863-The-Exclusive-Opera-Lively-Interview-with-Barbara-Hannigan

Christopher Purves

British baritone Christopher Purves created the role of The Protector in the world premiere in July of 2012 in Aix-en-Provence, and has since sung the role several times. In this context, we interviewed the talented and intelligent singer, who delivered some extremely insightful and interesting answers that are worth reading not only by those who are interested in contemporary opera, but by all opera lovers, in one of our best interviews to date.

He has appeared in five of the Written on Skin runs to date including the world premiere in Aix-en-Provence and also the Dutch National Opera, ROH Covent Garden, Opéra National de Paris, Bayerische Staatsoper in Munich, and Toulouse, and he has two more scheduled, including the first American staged performance of the opera in New York City (Lincoln Center Mostly Mozart Festival, August 11-13-15, 2015).

Luiz Gazzola for Opera Lively - Please explain to us how you view the psychology of the character The Protector in *Written on Skin*.

Christopher Purves - For me the psychology of the Protector is a simple matter at the beginning, in that he's sure of his life, he's strong and powerful, rich, safe and secure in his belief that his decisions will be obeyed and nothing will challenge his position. This is why when the boy is engaged to log the history of his powerful family, insecurity reigns. Not only does his wife start behaving differently but the boy's proximity seems to destabilize him as well. There is a frisson in the air that whilst not tangible, is felt equally by the Protector and Agnes. But unlike Agnes who receives the frisson with open eyes and heart and recognition, the Protector can't allow himself to get involved and doesn't know what to do with the change of atmosphere. He doesn't ask the questions, he doesn't know what to do with his new feelings and responds in his conditioned way by trying to suppress the emotions and those who've caused them.

OL - Any considerations to make about the scene in which The Protector seems to be erotically attracted to The Boy as well (right before he murders him)?

CP - I'm not sure that the Protector is necessarily attracted to the Boy in the same way that Agnes is. He doesn't understand the feelings he has for the Boy and responds in a way that is shocking for himself shocking for the Boy and the audience. I feel that it's an act of possession, making the Boy a part of his property and in a way subjugating him in the same way he has his wife. It was and continues to be a problematic scene for me as the Protector, as I never really saw the attraction for the Boy in the music and certainly in the text, but I suppose this is an instance where the production and directorial choice has informed the Protector's actions. I would love to see how other productions deal with this scene.

OL - Is the experience of interpreting a role such as The Protector which includes intense cruelty, in some way psychologically difficult for the performer? Does it get to be intense? Do you need to unwind after the show?

CP - Violence is a very important part of the Protector's character make-up, after all he's introduced by the Boy as being 'addicted to violence". The key to being able to depict this in the opera is to take away your own attitude as a person, as Chris, and start to think from another perspective. After that it all becomes a natural bedfellow to the Protector's character, he is always likely to respond to any challenge with violence, with aggression. Yes it was hard at the start to accept that the character I was to inhabit for the next two years was an unreconstructed loathsome creature who cared not a jot for the sentiments of normal folk and responded with ruthless violence to any change. Alcohol helps sometimes but also being with a cast who never judged me in any other way than as myself, really helped me experiment and take risks with the character.

OL - Tell us about the vocal challenges in singing this role. What parts are the biggest hurdles?

CP - The vocal challenges of the role amount to what you, as an actor, are prepared to put into the role. The role doesn't really make demands at the extremes of the voice but invite you to personalize the role in a way that few other roles do. I respond to the role in a way an actor might do to a text, I like to think, it's not always about making a beautiful noise, often the opposite. I try to shape the Protector's destruction with the use of every skill that I possess. I try to weep with the voice, to curse, to threaten, to exult, to tear, to rip, to cut, to cajole, to plead, to love even with my voice. Sometimes it works, sometimes it hurts, but I hope it serves the intentions of the composer and librettist- they haven't complained yet! I think that sometimes it's confusing for an audience who's used to singers always adopting a beautiful tone, to hear me challenge this opinion with noises that can only be described as animal, but it's a risk in my mind worth taking.

OL - What are your memories of opening night in Aix-en-Provence? Any interesting stories to tell about the before, during, and after?

CP - Opening night in Aix was for me incredibly special, as my then 15-year-old daughter was going to be in the audience. She's an experienced operagoer, but I was concerned how she was going to react to the scenes of intimacy with both Boy and Agnes, the violence and the modernity of the piece. I met a lot of people from the operatic world beforehand, all eagerly awaiting the talk of the town and indeed the talk of the operatic community. I know we didn't disappoint, and my daughter still mentions the performance as one she'll never forget.

OL - You have now created a role in an opera that has been heralded as one of the best works of the last several decades, which is likely to have lasting power and to be regarded by musicologists, critics, and the public in the next century, when they look back, as one of the operatic peaks in history. This is akin to some immortality. How do you feel about it?

CP - To be involved in any creation in art is an unbelievable privilege, and this Opera which we recognized as a masterpiece is no different. As a relative unknown in contemporary music, and unknown in

Europe, I came to the production with rather a lot to prove, a lot of people had put faith in me for which I'll always be incredibly grateful. To make musical history is something to tell my grandchildren, but to be part of the initial process from which this production has taken shape is a gift that I do not take lightly.

OL - How were you picked by Benjamin for the role?

CP - I'm fairly sure that George had looked at a few other baritones before he came to me. I was recommended by a mutual and trusted friend who obviously sold me very well. We met up at his house in London and sang through most of the rep that I knew, with George accompanying me on the piano. We sang *Wozzeck*, *Falstaff*, Handel and Bach, works from composers very close to my heart. I don't know why he stopped his search with me, but by God am I glad he did.

OL - Please describe the process of creating the role with Mr. Benjamin, Mr. Crimp, and Ms. Mitchell.

CP - The process of putting flesh on to the character with George and Martin and Katie, and of course the rest of the cast was an agonizing one. What choices do you make? No one has done it before so there's nowhere to go for clues. Martin's response was in many ways rather like his text; a little ambiguous, a little too profound, but always very respectful of the choices I found myself making. George was so utterly helpful likewise, so protective of his magnificent score and yet so tolerant of the course I was steering. But with so much of great art, so much clarity comes from understanding the context, the intention, and there are enough 'signposts' along the way to provide answers to your searching questions.

OL - Considering your performances of this role in five

different occasions – Aix-en-Provence, DNO, Covent Garden, Bayerische, and Toulouse, would you please describe briefly differences in staging and public reaction in these five runs?

CP - I suppose the audience appreciation has grown with our own growth as performers of this Opera. Certainly in Aix the reception was ecstatic as of course they and we were witnessing this work for the first giddy time. As performers have slipped seamlessly in and out, myself included, the standard has remained at the highest level. All the orchestras we've encountered have risen gloriously to the challenge, and I can safely say that the reception we received at the Opéra Comique in Paris, was just incredible.

OL - You've performed very well the title role in Wozzeck. It has some similitude to Written on Skin. How do you compare the two operas, and the two roles, musically, dramatically and vocally?

CP - You ask me to compare my two favorite roles, The Protector and Wozzeck, God I'm just so lucky to have been able to sing them both. Wozzeck is a harder challenge vocally as it takes in the extremes of my voice (top Bb to bottom C, just under the three octaves!) and asks the performer to be blown about, emotionally, like a small boat in the ocean. The Protector is in many ways the Ocean to Wozzeck's boat, he is the bully, the oppressor. But both roles ask you to inhabit the mind of someone so different to oneself. In many ways I use the same performing technique for both roles, I set my brain as a blank piece of paper with no preconceptions no thoughts no external interruptions, and sing the words of Crimp and Buchner to the best of my ability, using the imagination that I've refined over the years. I suppose in crude terms both operas last about 1hr 45mins and have 15 scenes a death and a suicide at the end, and I'd still like to be singing them until I die.

OL - Another role and opera that would be interesting to contrast and compare to The Protector and *Written on Skin* would be Golaud in *Pelléas et Mélisande* which is also in your repertory. Please tell us about it, just like in the question above.

CP - When I first read through *Written on Skin* I had a feeling I'd travelled this road before. Golaud is also a man who finds that insecurity is a very destructive force, and a lack of absolute certainty can lead to ruin. Neither man can cope with change, neither man can open himself to the possibility of a different life to the one he lives, and neither man can trust the influence of the outsider. It seems that I'm destined to play closed, scared and oppressive men. Real life mirroring art and vice versa?

OL - You have an impressive range of styles, having performed from Baroque such as Handel's *Acis and Galatea* and *Alcina* all the way to contemporary *Written on Skin*. What period of operatic production you feel is the most comfortable for you?

CP - My love of Baroque opera and music in general comes from the feeling that it's very much up to the performer how to interpret the character of the music. Now that Baroque music has been liberated from the hands of the "authentic" police (tongue in cheek) we performers feel that in a way the roles are a blank canvas onto which we can paint away with imagination allied to decorum. I can't think of anything better than performing the aria from Bach's *St. Matthew Passion*, "Mache dich mein herze rein," with the knowledge that the conductor is allowing me to use my musical imagination to tell a personal story rather than being a little hidebound by some historical rules and practices. For as long as I have a voice I'll always want to mix Baroque and Benjamin.

OL - How do you see the possibilities of contemporary opera, in terms of seducing the public? Do you think younger audiences such as teenagers and young adults are more likely to engage with contemporary opera, or with modernly staged ancient opera (including the use of modern imagery technology), or with plain traditionally staged ancient opera – or does it matter?

CP - I really do think that in opera in general we have to ask ourselves what do we think that the audience responds to best, what will keep this wonderful art form alive? For me it's simple. Hearing Barbara Hannigan scream with every sinew of her body, the last note to scene 10 of *Written on Skin* is about as close as you get to experiencing what it is to feel an emotion. You are left in no doubt that she is about pain, revenge, hatred and so much more besides. It's that directness and unabashed commitment to the delivery of human emotion, that, no matter the format, the audience can relate to. The frustration, the damage, the hatred of that note is heard the world over, and it's so human. I do believe that as soon as you take the human quality out of Opera, and it becomes a chess game of ideas and pictures and attitudes, you lose the audience that it was written for. The human voice is so powerful not just in decibels but in nuance in suggestion in all its subtleties, that an audience whether it's watching modern opera or modern reconstructions of older opera needs it as the centerpiece. I think as soon as the voice becomes a subsidiary to the 'Concept' then as an art form it's lost.

OL - Most of your roles require strong acting skills, which you do have. How have you acquired your solid acting?

CP - Acting for me is adapting your own sensibilities to

suit the character you're portraying, then add in a very liberal amount of imagination, humor, and insight and observation, and you're there. I've never had any formal training whatsoever, I never went to music college or conservatoire, I've just watched and watched and adopted certain traits from other folk into my own life and handed them all over to whatever character I'm supposed to be.

OL - You returned in April 2014 to Houston Grand Opera for your first Alberich in the *Das Rheingold*. Is this something you approached with trepidation? Are you planning to plant a solid foothold in Wagner (Beckmesser is also in your repertory), or to remain eclectic (sometimes Wagnerian singers tend to be type-cast)?

CP - I've loved my Wagner experiences, I've found the roles of Beckmesser and Alberich almost impossible to get to grips with, but over time and with some of the finest nurturing talents around, take a bow Anthony Negus at WNO and Kathleen Kelly at HGO, I've come through on the other side. But to limit myself now to Wagner would be to ignore the challenges of Written of Skin and Handel and Verdi and Mozart, the list goes on and on. No, I'll never stop with Wagner; there's too much great music to discover.

OL - If you are at a liberty to say, will you be in the Lincoln Center American staged premiere of Written on Skin in August 2015? (I do know you'll be in the Canadian concert premiere in Toronto).

CP - Yes I'll be there in NY, you bet!

OL - Please if you don't mind let's switch a bit to the man underneath the artist, so that our readers get to know you a bit more. How was your encounter with classical music in general, and opera in particular, growing up?

CP - I was in choirs all my life so I'm steeped and indeed pickled in classical music. It's only a short hop to opera, especially when you throw in a desire to show off, wear strange clothes and pretend to be someone else and, as fourth son of four boys, a desire to be noticed by my parents. Oh and I like to be loud and the drug of singing is a very powerful one.

OL - How do you describe your take in life and personality?

CP - I like to think of myself as a calmish person, witty, irreverent, cheeky, kind, attentive, caring and loving to those who I know intimately and to new colleagues alike. I have some horrid demons in my life, don't we all, these help me and hinder me in equal measure, but I do happen to have such a beautiful family to help me, and the most long-suffering and intuitive, beautiful wife who shows me the way to go.

OL - What are some of your extra-musical interests, passions, and/or hobbies?

CP - Outside of musical life I have my wife and family of three gorgeous children, a girl and two boys, who take up all my time. I play field hockey and football and golf with my boys and we've just come back from the most incredible surf driven holiday in Australia with my best friend from school. My daughter is a very good flautist so a lot of time at home is spent taking her to this lesson that orchestra and the other conservatoire. I have a great dog called Stanley who needs huge attention when I'm home and of course I like to drink beer in pubs.

OL - OK, that was our last question.

CP - Thanks for such interesting questions, I could have

said ten times as much.

OL - Thank you for your very insightful answers; I believe our readers will love them.

This interview is also featured online on Operalively.com, with complete artistic biography, discography, pictures and video clips. Type the following URL on your browser:

http://operalively.com/forums/content.php/952-The-Exclusive-Opera-Lively-Interview-with-Christopher-Purves

Tim Mead

We interviewed countertenor Tim Mead who performed the roles of The Boy/First Angel in two runs of the opera (Toulouse and Lisbon) and will be singing these roles again in New York City in August 2015 (Mostly Mozart Festival).

Luiz Gazzola for Opera Lively - Please explain to us how you view the psychology of the character The Boy in Written on Skin.

Tim Mead - When we first meet the Boy he is an ambiguous and unnerving presence. There's a purity in his outward appearance that provides an almost blank canvas, onto which the suspicions of others are easily painted. But one thing is certain, there is something within this mysterious stranger that draws everyone irresistibly and tragically towards him.

He is a carefully drawn character, who reveals himself little by little, holding our fascination throughout. What strikes me most about the Boy is that he maintains a certain cold detachment throughout the story - his seemingly insolent responses to his employers, his icy manipulation/seduction of Agnes, the ease of his lies in his confrontation with the Protector. Most telling, perhaps, is the conclusion of the scene in which he presents the finished book containing the secret page that condemns Agnes: "My work – smiles the Boy – is done". This is a character who has clearly taken some pleasure from turning this small, sheltered family unit upside down.

Because of this, it's hard to develop much sympathy for him. But herein lies the conflict. He produces these ravishingly drawn pages and speaks/sings with such purity and beauty that we find ourselves under his spell. The sympathy really lies with the Angel who plays him. The Angel, who wishes to experience humanity to find meaning to existence, yet sees such pain and unhappiness, ending with the awful reality of a gruesome death.

OL - Any considerations to make about the scene in which The Protector seems to be erotically attracted to The Boy as well (right before he murders him)?

TM - I would say that The Protector only 'seems' to be erotically attracted to The Boy. I've never viewed this scene as being sexually motivated.

There is a suffocating tension in this confrontation, which feels quite unbearable in performance. The Protector is clearly affected by the Boy in ways he may not understand and feels the need to take control of the situation through reasserting his sense of ownership of him. This is the first point in which these two manipulators are faced by a situation in which neither of them is in control.

To break the tension of the scene with a kiss is strong statement that surprises both the characters and audience alike. I've always found the strangely intense music that follows the kiss an opportunity to allow the character of the Angel to break through the shell of the Boy he is playing. It is a feeling of shock, surprise, even a sense of pity for the Protector that he has been pushed to this point and one of relief that the knife, so prominent in the opening of the scene, has not been used to engineer his end.

I'm sure that all of us who have played the scene have viewed it slightly differently. But this is one of the joys of a role being interpreted by a number of different artists and what ultimately gives any piece of work life.

OL - Is the experience of interpreting a role such as The Boy, which includes a fairly long psychological arc, in some way psychologically difficult for the performer? Does it get to be intense? Do you need to unwind after the show?

TM - One of the things I really enjoyed about playing the role in Katie's production is that the character of the Boy is on stage at all times. You have no choice but to be immersed in the role from the first notes until the final chord. Such continued focus in such an intense piece of work is, obviously, exhausting. But I'm not sure that I'd want it any other way!

In watching back the DVD taken from the Covent Garden run I was interested to experience the strength of my reactions to some of the most intense moments of the work. That this feeling still exists is testament to the power of the opera and this production.

Of course, you need to unwind after any performance, especially one as intense as this, but that's nothing a few pints with some friendly faces can't fix!

OL - Tell us about the vocal challenges in singing this role. What is the range? Is it difficult to learn? What parts are the biggest hurdles?

TM - For the most part, the role sits in the middle to the bottom of my voice. Excursions to the upper extremes of the voice are reserved for moments of highest drama (for example, the scene in which Agnes accuses the Boy of lying). So in terms of range, it's a fairly comfortable sing. George's orchestration is incredibly sensitive, so the singer never feels challenged by the orchestra. All these factors really help the singer to deliver the music and text in as naturalistic a way as possible.

The music is far from simple, but because George's music responds so instinctively to the contours and rhythm of Martin Crimp's libretto it seems to cement itself in the brain with surprising ease, as if there were no other way of singing these words.

What is very challenging is trying to reproduce all the small detail that George has lovingly put into his score. The slightest subtlety of rhythm or dynamic might not seem such a big deal but is absolutely vital to the naturalism or the color of the line. George has never settled for anything less than total accuracy when I've worked with him on it. While this can make rehearsal grueling at times, the benefits of this sort of attention to detail are huge when it comes to live performance. He really has given us everything we need to paint these characters and tell this story.

OL - The role was created for another countertenor, Mr. Bejun Mehta. Was there any needed adaptation when you sang the role, or are your ranges very similar?

TM - I think that Bejun and I have similar ranges and George certainly didn't need to make any adjustments for me. Bejun has real strength at the bottom of his voice and George has clearly exploited this in the way he has written the role, with frequent dips to the very bottom of the range. This will make the role unsuitable for some countertenors, but I didn't find it to be a problem. Whilst Bejun and I have quite different sounding voices, I think the role works equally well for both of us. It's a role that I feel fits my voice and artistic personality as well as if it had been written with me in mind. For me, it really is a gift of a role.

OL - Did you watch the video recording of the world premiere in Aix-en-Provence (at the time, available on Medici TV on pay-per-view) before you sang the role? If yes, how did you plan your performance; any different take from your predecessor's?

TM - Before the rehearsals in Toulouse I watched the video from Aix repeatedly. I also went to see a performance during the run in Amsterdam. It was really important that I was able to absorb as much of the production's detail as possible before rehearsals began, as rehearsal time in Toulouse was very limited. Fortunately for me, Bejun is a very clear performer and I was able to understand much of what the role required. The important thing in these situations is to take as much information as possible about the production from your predecessor in the role without becoming a mimic.

My natural instinct with the role was to focus on the incredible beauty George had written into it, and to use the sound of the words and musical line to seduce and affect the course of the story, rather than impose myself in a more physical way. I felt it important that the other characters were drawn to the Boy in a way that was subtle and quiet, but unavoidable.

My performance is, obviously, based on the great work that Bejun did at Aix in creating the role, but I'm sure our performances are different. We are different people, so our performances are naturally colored by our different personalities.

OL - Considering your performances of this role in two different occasions – in Lisbon and Toulouse, would you please describe briefly any differences in public reaction in these two runs? Maybe there were no differences.

TM - My experience of performing this opera (both the fully staged production in Toulouse and the semi-staged version in Lisbon) is that audiences appear to be gripped by the music and the story from the very start. As a performer I've sensed very little restlessness amongst the audience, which suggests a high level of attention and concentration. Feeling that sort of concentration from your audience only helps fuel the focus of those on stage.

OL - What is the feeling you have, as an artist, regarding being part of the first few runs of such a formidable contemporary masterpiece like Written on Skin?

TM - From my very first encounter with the production I was fascinated by the score and the story it told. Something about it really spoke to me as an artist.

Taking my place amongst such a wonderful cast was a particular joy. The high level at which Barbara Hannigan and Chris Purves operate, both vocally and dramatically, was incredible to experience at such close quarters. My scenes with both of them easily rank amongst the most intense and dramatically satisfying moments of my career so far.

I just feel very fortunate to be part of such an incredible piece of work and to be given the opportunity to share it with audiences, many of whom will be experiencing it for the first time. I already see it as one of the real highlights of my artistic life and, were I to sing for 50 years more, I'm sure this wouldn't change.

OL - When you revisit the role, is there anything you are planning to change in your performance?

TM - For me, it's a case of continuing to learn more about the character and striving to convey all the wonderful detail that George has written. Finding that aspect of the Boy's character that is quietly irresistible is a constant challenge. I'm hoping that it will also offer me the chance to work with Katie more directly (as yet, we've only had the opportunity to discuss the role/production rather than work on it in the rehearsal studio).

OL - Now, let's move on from this piece and address other parts of your career, since this interview won't be used exclusively for the Written on Skin guidebook but will also appear on our website, for the general public. So, here we go: We have interviewed maestro Leon Botstein who expressed an opinion similar to that of the late Sir Colin Davis, arguing that historically informed orchestras using period instruments are what he called "creative history" since nobody can really know how the orchestras really sounded back then, which would be akin to redesigning an ancient vase from a small fragment. He sustains that modern orchestras shouldn't be bumped out of the Baroque repertoire under what he believes is a somewhat arrogant stance from the HIP orchestras that pretend that they know best. On the other end of the spectrum there is Vivica Genaux who also granted us an interview, saying that she loves HIP orchestras and ensembles so much that she wishes that even more recent music could be played on period instruments. Where do you situate yourself in this controversy?

TM - All the views you've offered in your question are equally valid. The most important thing is that talented artists with a love of this repertoire and a desire to communicate it are able to perform it. The idea that any particular group of musicians should 'own' corners of the repertoire is ridiculous! As with most things in music, there is no right way to do anything and it is the variety of approach that keeps things interesting!

The many great baroque ensembles on the scene today offer vivid and delicately nuanced performances, informed by research, but not dictated by it. Within their relatively modest proportions, music making is intimate and full of the sort of detail that might get lost in larger ensembles.

This isn't to say that this music doesn't benefit from performances by larger, modern orchestras. Such ensembles are used to playing a range of different styles, so there is no reason why they shouldn't be able to adapt their playing to the requirements of the Baroque. It is rare that I get the opportunity to perform with modern orchestras, one recent example being a run of *Messiah* with the New York Philharmonic. With my ears tuned to the sound of period instruments, I find experiences such as this fascinating. It's like seeing the music through a different lens. They also present me with the opportunity to work with great musicians that I might never have contact with if I stayed within the confines of the Historical Informed world.

OL - Countertenors have a natural placement in Baroque, but are increasingly featured in contemporary opera as well. You have extensive Baroque experience but you are now being featured in these contemporary pieces. What period of operatic production you feel is the most comfortable for you? How do you compare them, for the performer? For example, you do a lot of Handel but then you did Birtwistle's *The Minotaur* (an opera I love); would you compare and contrast these eras, for the countertenor?

TM - The countertenor will always have his operatic home in the baroque period. I feel fortunate that I've been able to focus so much of my energy on one period, allowing me a far deeper understanding of the style than I might have achieved if my concentration had been spread across a broader spectrum of music. Other singers often comment that I must get bored of singing baroque music all the time, but I've never felt this way. I've always found great variety within the genre. I really don't see how you can consider Monteverdi and Handel to be 'the same sort of thing'. Opera of this period provides the performer with huge interpretative scope. Other than the basic notes on the page, the composer tends to leave few other directions as to how the music is to be performed. With a composer that I know well, such as Handel, I find myself constantly looking for clues within the score to inform my interpretation of, not only the music, but the operatic characters he is portraying. There are always a multitude of answers and constructing a complete interpretation of a role is a never-ending process.

There's no doubting that, however flamboyant the written vocal line or ornamentation applied to it may be, singing baroque music requires considerable vocal control. The moment I sing contemporary music, I feel a certain degree of freedom. I feel freed from the deftly crafted shapes that give baroque music its distinctive character. It could also be the case that I feel freed from the burden of stylistic information that I have accumulated in my years of singing music of the 17th century. Contemporary music helps me explore other aspects of my musical personality and allows me to express myself in different ways.

What binds the very earliest opera with the most contemporary work is the importance and focus on text and the desire to communicate the words of a story as well as make beautiful noises. Maybe this is why many artists (not just countertenors) find themselves specializing in both eras.

The problem I find with much of the contemporary writing for the countertenor is that so much of it sits at the very top of the vocal range. This leads to parts that can be ungrateful and amount to little more than sustained screaming! This is why the role in 'Written on Skin' is such a welcome addition to the countertenor repertoire. Whilst notes at the upper extremes of the voice might be thrilling to hear, they provide little opportunity for the singer to communicate his full palette of colors and emotions.

Being involved in the premiere of Birtwistle's *The Minotaur* was a great experience (and an event that also marked my debut at the Royal Opera, Covent Garden!). Harrison was with us for the whole rehearsal process, providing insight where necessary whilst allowing the artists to discover the score for themselves. My overriding memory of the work is the elemental force that fills the orchestra pit. Birtwistle certainly holds nothing back in his creation of the labyrinth. In the end, my role as Innocent number 5 wasn't so extensive, but it was wonderful to see such a significant opera premiere showcase the countertenor voice in 3 roles.

OL - Italian and English opera, especially, favored the use of castrati. Obviously, for all our efforts at historical authenticity, this is one element truly beyond our scope. What are your thoughts then with regards to the use of female singers vs. young choir boys vs. countertenors?

TM - I don't really have a preference when it comes to who sings what, although for the purposes of self-preservation I'm probably supposed to say that only countertenors should be cast to sing the castrati roles! The most important thing is that we have the best artists for the job. In this respect, that is the authentic option. Handel seems to have used the best of the vocal resources available to him at any given time, using both castrati and mezzos or even rewriting parts for different vocal ranges, substituting singers as the circumstances required. There are plenty of countertenors today who sound like mezzos and vice versa, so I'm not sure that it's always an issue of the timbre of the voice.

However, when casting a baroque opera I think it's important that every effort is made to provide a varied and distinctive palette of vocal timbre to define the characters. Often a cast full of countertenors in castrati roles may be less interesting than if some of these roles were to be assigned to mezzos.

The issue of gender is, perhaps, now more a theatrical issue. There have been some wonderfully insightful baroque productions that really make this type of opera as natural as you could hope for. Some feel that trouser roles work less well in this kind of setting. I guess it's a personal preference. I think most people would prefer to have the role performed well than cast on the basis of gender or a preference for once voice category over another.

OL - On the same token, how do countertenors produce their sound?

TM - I don't really think that the basics of how we produce sound are that different from any other voice type. Most male singers will possess some form of head voice or falsetto, it's just that we countertenors have chosen to develop and strengthen this part of the voice.

OL - After the strong Handel operatic revival, we've been seeing more operas by Vivaldi (you've done one, *L'Olympiade*, and the occasional other operatic work from the period). What works and composers you'd like to see revived?

TM - I'd love to do more Cavalli! Having performed Endimione in *La Calisto* at the Bayerische Staatsoper in Munich and Paggio in *Ercole Amante* in Amsterdam, I'm always struck by the beauty and creativeness of his writing. Theatrically he has the same sort of immediacy as Monteverdi but with greater opportunity for more lyrical reflections.

Fortunately I have a new Cavalli production in the diary for the 2015/16 season, *Xerxes*. I've recently got a taste for the operas of Francesco Conti and have recording plans for *L'Issipile* with La Nuova Musica under their fantastic young director (and my good friend!), David Bates. Having done some initial work on a few of the arias I'm excited by the possibilities of his music. It's similar in style to Handel, with some surprises! He seems to have particular skill in painting characters through music, so I'm looking forward to exploring his work in more depth.

One of the biggest problems with reviving forgotten operas is finding works that are consistently high in quality and do not just rely on one or two stand-out arias. In terms of staging it's also important to have a plot that stands up to theatrical treatment. Too many librettos are convoluted nonsense and are difficult to make sense of, let alone make relevant for a modern audience. In some cases it might be preferable to cherry pick the best arias and use them as show pieces rather than attempt full operas.

OL - What do you like best, and why – performing a cycle of songs or a song mix in a recital, performing in an oratorio or concert opera, or a fully staged opera? What are particular challenges of each of these modalities?

TM - I don't really have a preference. I've always felt that a balance between all forms of performance is important, as each informs the other. At the start of my career I was almost exclusively involved in staged operas. This was great as it gave me some much needed time to concentrate on my stagecraft and work as an actor.

I remember coming back to Handel's Messiah (now a regular fixture in my schedule and a recent CD release) after years of opera and finding so much more dramatic sense in it than I had during my time as a student. I also think that the exposed and intimate nature of the recital platform brings story-telling into sharp focus, which can only be a plus when you return to telling stories on the much larger scale of an opera stage.

OL - Who do you look up to, in the world of countertenor singing?

TM - I have to confess to being something of a countertenor geek with a CD collection stacked full of discs by a variety of singers, which I think is a common occurrence in the world of countertenor singing!

While I was an undergraduate, I was absolutely obsessed with the Bach cantata recordings of Andreas Scholl. The elegance of his singing is something that I have always prized. Having now had the opportunity to perform alongside him, I'm struck by what an instinctive, musical and generous artist he is.

I grew to admire the work of David Daniels slightly later. This probably coincided with a shift in my own focus from concert to operatic repertoire. One of the most informative experiences of my early career was to understudy David in the title role of Cesare at Glyndebourne. Watching him rehearse taught me so much about what it is to do this job and how to navigate such lengthy roles. Listening to him sing 'Aure, deh, per pieta' within the intimate confines of a rehearsal room was a moment I felt privileged to experience.

More recently I've been drawn to the work of Bejun Mehta, Lawrence Zazzo and Christophe Dumaux. All these artists show such commitment to using their voices in service of the dramatic intentions of the music. I admire them for their willingness to take risks and inhabit roles so fully. In the hands of such artists, the countertenor voice can no longer be perceived as merely a vehicle for pretty noises.

I often find myself looking up repertoire and being surprised and inspired by a vast array of different countertenor voices: the delicacy of line Alfred Deller brings to a Robert Johnson song, the emotional intelligence with which Michael Chance delivers Dowland, the simple beauty with which Dominique Visse (a wonderful colleague, more known for his comic roles) sings a lullaby and many, many more, too numerous to mention.

Above all I admire the two countertenors that I've been fortunate enough to have as teachers, Charles Brett and Robin Blaze. For their music, their invaluable wisdom and advice, and, above all, their patience with me, a most impatient student!

OL - Andreas Scholl has recorded J.S. Bach's cantata *Ich habe genug* BWV 82, originally scored for bass, while Philippe Jaroussky recorded a disc of 19th century French mélodie by Faure, Debussy, etc... Do you have any plans to perform works outside the usual realm of the countertenor?

TM - Over the years I've often sung German lieder (Schubert, Schumann and Brahms) as well as English art song. I've never really considered this to be particularly unusual, given that when I was a student countertenor David Daniels was performing and recording this sort of repertoire regularly. I believe that I'm the only countertenor to have recorded the Brahms *Liebeslieder Waltzes*, but I'm sure I'll not be the only one for very long!

I'm always open to trying repertoire that might be slightly unexpected for countertenors. It's a case of being honest about what you can sing and what suits you. Just because you are physically able to sing the notes of a piece doesn't necessarily mean you should!

OL - You are featured in two DVDs of *Admeto*. I confess that I have mixed feelings about how successful the Japanese Samurai theme was, in Doris Dörrie's production for which you sang the title role. You were Trasimede in the one directed by Axel Köhler, which updates the opera to a modern hospital. Please contrast and compare the two productions, and tell us what you think of the directorial efforts to present Handel in creative and original ways. How should Handel's operas be staged? (I usually like updates but sometimes I feel a little dizzy with all the extremes and all the wild settings these directors employ with Handel and I almost crave a traditionally staged one – what is up with Handel that attracts all these Regie productions?)

TM - Given that *Admeto* is fairly unknown and rarely performed it's rather surprising that I've been involved in 2 staged productions and 2 recordings of the opera. (There are only 3 recordings of the work, so I'm on 66% of them!).

Any attempt to update Handel's operas in a way that helps in the telling of the story is a good thing. To date, I've only been involved in one 'period' production, which probably reflects the current fashion for modern productions in Europe rather than what is necessarily 'best' for the material. The human stories that these operas tell can be clearly portrayed whatever the setting, costuming or governing concept, as long as the story is at the heart of all the directorial decisions made.

These two *Admeto* productions are markedly different. Axel Kohler's updating is actually quite straightforward. A hospital is an obvious place to locate the drama as the opera opens with *Admeto* on his deathbed. Within this realistic setting the family drama plays out in a quite natural way, with the slightly curious addition of baroque-style gesture in some of the arias, the whole thing being colored by Axel's particularly infectious humor!

Doris Dörrie, on the other hand, offered something incredibly stylized. Doris has a great fascination with Japan, the samurai and the movement of butoh. The physical language that this imposed on the production was very interesting. We spent many afternoons in butoh workshops working on the movement that would inform the physicality of the whole production. As the process continued I began to see parallels between this micro-control of movement (so central to butoh) and the gestural language of baroque theatre. In fact, Doris saw this as a period piece, in that she located the production in the baroque period, but in Japan not Europe. I found it fascinating to define a character so clearly through movement.

OL - You also had two DVDs of *L'Incoronazione di Poppea*, both in the role of Ottone, one at Den Norske Opera and the other one at Opéra de Lille. The former was a quite, let's say, bloody one (laughs…), and the latter had a mix of ancient and contemporary costumes. Again, please contrast and compare these two approaches to the piece. The former was visually interesting in my opinion, with the contrasting colors white, red, and black. The latter was theatrically intriguing.

TM - This opera, and the role of Ottone, has been central to my career from the very start. Having made my professional debut in the role at the Opéra de Lyon in 2005 under William Christie, I went on to create new productions at English National Opera, Den Norske Opera, Opéra de Lille and Opéra de Dijon (and I'm sure there will be more new productions in my future!) As a result it's been the role that has occupied my thoughts the most over the years.

It's a very difficult opera to stage and few productions are fully satisfying. There is just so much detail in the music and libretto that it has to be rehearsed as if a piece of straight theatre. There is absolutely no place in the score where standing at the front and simply singing beautifully will be anywhere near enough.

The two productions that I've recorded, I love. Working with Ole Anders Tandberg in Oslo was a complete joy. He treated the libretto like Shakespeare and wouldn't let any detail pass. Together we developed the sort of Ottone that had been forming in my mind for some time. It's a characterization that focuses on his strengths rather than his weaknesses and vulnerability. The desperate situation the character finds himself in from the first few pages often leads to interpretations that show him to be a whiner and a wimp. But this man is a decorated soldier recently returned from war, who has enough about him to attract the affections of the much-desired Poppea. So at every turn we looked to deliver his complaints as challenges to his situation. He remained the fighter in love that he was on the battlefield. On watching back the results some years later, I have to say, the character we created was a very angry man! Perhaps we took it too far, but this experience has certainly strengthened my subsequent interpretations.

The production in Lille was a more sensitive affair. Jean Francois Sivadier is a wonderful actor/director and we worked again at revising my characterization of Ottone. What I wanted to achieve here (following the Oslo production) was to find a way to reintegrate some of Ottone's beauty, to make him someone that we could believe Poppea would genuinely have fallen in love with (believing, against the norm, that Poppea is a character capable of genuine love). We hoped to use this as a balance to his strength and anger and make a character with whom we have a chance of feeling some sympathy. As is so often the case, the clues to how we might do this lay in the music Monteverdi has written and Emmanuelle Haim was the perfect musical partner to guide and shape this detail. There was something very natural about this production and the character relationships that we created that will stay with me each time I play Ottone in the future.

OL - That *Ercole Amante* by DNO was lots of fun. Any interesting memories of that production?

TM - It was a fun production! I'm glad it comes across so

well on the DVD. David Alden really let his incredible imagination go wild with this one. There were so many fantastical ideas that eventually didn't make it into the show and, as you can see, the show is stuffed full of them! I wonder how the opera would work without such imaginative stage direction…

OL - I'm very impressed with your discography, with 29 items, by a still quite young singer (you are 33, right?). How did you manage to be so prolific? What are the pieces you like best in your discography/videography, and why?

TM - Ha! Yes, I am 33. But seeing as I made my professional operatic debut at the age of 23, I guess I've been around a bit longer than many other singers my age.

I'm often surprised at the size of my discography too! It's certainly not the norm these days, so I feel incredibly fortunate to have been given the opportunity to record so frequently.

Like many artists, I'm not sure I love any of my recordings. I find it impossible to listen to any of my work without criticizing the minutest details. So I will leave it to other ears to judge what they might consider the best!

What I am proud of is that I've recorded many works that have either never been recorded or have been recorded very rarely, such as Cavalli's Ercole Amante, Handel's *Flavio, Riccardo Primo, Admeto, Triumph of Time and Truth*, JC Smith's *Paradise Lost* and *The Seasons*.

My overly critical ear is generally more pleased with my most recent work, which I guess is obvious seeing as I'm constantly striving to progress. But I'm often surprised on occasional hearings of my earlier recordings at the slightly less refined freedom of my 'youth' and there is definitely some merit in that. In my retirement I'm sure I'll be glad to be able to see this record of my journey as a singer and an artist preserved on disc.

OL - Let's talk future performances a bit. Do you look forward to Glass' *Akhnaten* at Vlaamse Opera in 2015? What do you think of his music? (I personally love it).

TM - I'm preparing *Akhnaten* right now. I can't say that I had much exposure to Glass' work before this project came along. At the moment I'm listening to passages of the opera regularly to help me become more acquainted with his musical world. The thing that really strikes me is that the music constantly conjures images in my mind. I see endless possibilities for the staging of this music and I really can't wait to see what the director, Nigel Lowrey, has in store for us! There's a relentless nature to the score that propels the story along, emphasizing that time passes whether you pay attention to it or not. But there are also moments of real beauty. The scenes between Akhnaten and his wife may initially appear to be rather cold and clinical, but in the formal structures of their interweaving lines you hear and feel a couple existing completely as one. It's the purity of their union that is so striking.

This is one of the projects that I'm most looking forward to as I see it as something totally different from anything I've done before, both musically and theatrically.

OL - Then you'll be in Saint Louis for *Riccardo Primo*. I like the director very much, Lee Blakely. I shall try to attend it. Anything to tell us about that one?

TM - It's an opera that I've previously performed in concert and recorded, although in the secondary role of Oronte. I don't yet know anything about the production. But in a more idle moment the other day, I was googling images of Richard I and I noticed he shares a remarkable likeness to my bearded self... so maybe it's time to ditch the razor again!

I worked with Lee years ago while I was understudying on David McVicar's *Giulio Cesare* at Glyndebourne, so it will be great to be reunited! The conductor, Christian Curnyn, is someone I have worked with a great deal over the years. Christian has a keen sense of what is required to communicate the drama of baroque opera in an unfussy and natural way, so I'm looking forward to creating something interesting with him. This is a US premiere, which is always exciting, showing an audience something new.

OL - Finally, another world premiere - the title role of Theo Loevendie's *The Rise of Spinoza* at the Concertgebouw. Please tell us about this one.

TM - A major new role for the countertenor voice is always welcome, and to have some involvement in its creation was fantastic. I met with Theo when the opera was still a series of sketches and we went through it all, seeing how his music fit my voice. He was incredibly sensitive and accommodating of my requirements.

The work is relatively short and its four scenes cover the climactic moments of the life of the philosopher Baruch Spinoza. Loevendie's music creates varying landscapes, from a bustling market place to the more intimate setting of Spinoza's study, with big philosophical questions being balanced with more personal moments.

The premiere was a concert performance, in front of an enthusiastic, sold out Concertgebouw audience. I know that Theo envisages a staged production and it will be interesting to see how the work develops once it's in a theatre.

OL - As a choral scholar at King's College, Cambridge, you studied musicology. How did your academic pursuits influence you as a singer and performer?

TM - My time at Cambridge has had a huge influence on everything I've done since, although I'm not sure how much of this is due to my academic pursuits. Very little of my study focused on the Baroque repertoire that forms the basis of my career.

I took all sorts of courses during my time there, finding myself drawn to those that weren't necessarily focused 100% on the music. Courses such as 'Music and Politics in Soviet Russia', 'Music and the English Reformation', 'The representation of music in art' and 'Notation in 13th century France' (my personal favorite!) provided a more rounded education than a more practical course of study might have. Opera is about so much more than just singing and music, so any study that broadens horizons is clearly of benefit.

OL - Why did you switch from cello and piano to operatic singing? In what way does your cello and piano background inform your singing?

TM - It wasn't really the case that I made a conscious decision to stop being a cellist/pianist and become a singer. Up until the time I began my undergraduate degree I was primarily a cellist, but with the commitment required by the choir at King's, Cambridge there left little time for my cello playing. In any case, it was becoming clear to me that singing was to be a far more serious part of my life.

I think you can always tell a singer who has an instrumental background from one who hasn't. The years spent in orchestras playing amongst so many musicians or within the more intimate surroundings of a string quartet really hone your skills as a collaborative musician, rather than someone who just stands out the front and does their own thing.

OL - Please if you don't mind let's switch a bit to the man underneath the artist, so that our readers get to know you a bit more. How was your encounter with classical music in general, and opera in particular, growing up? Where you from a musical family?

TM - I'm not from a particularly musical family, although neither of my parents were very shy about singing around the house at the top of their voices!

Like many children, I started playing the recorder at an early age and was a chorister at my local cathedral in Chelmsford by the time I was 7. From there I went on to study piano, cello and oboe, as well as trying my hand at any instrument that happened to be lying around!

I got my first taste of opera at the age of 12 when I was asked to sing the role of the Spirit of the Boy in Britten's *Curlew River* at the Royal Scottish Academy and on tour in Japan, under the late Sir Philip Ledger. It's a small role within this chamber scale piece, but it's full of intensity. It was a totally new experience for me to be on stage and in costume under the glare of the lights. I remember enjoying the experience very much. But after it was over I returned to my other musical studies, certain that focusing on my cello was the most useful thing for me to do.

It wasn't until I was at university that I really gave opera another thought and sang in some plucky student productions of *Cesare* and Stradella's *San Giovanni Battista*. But it was really only after I saw professional productions in London when I was coming to the end of my undergraduate days that I was gripped by the excitement of what opera could be.

OL - How do you describe your take on life and personality?

TM - I probably take life a little too seriously at times, whilst being prone to regular bouts of silliness, which probably sums up what colleagues see of me in the rehearsal studio! I've always been rather shy, a trait that is necessarily swallowed up once you're on stage, but is still definitely part of my personality, and one that people often misinterpret!

I do think of a few more things to say in answer to this question, but then I won't, because I'd be sounding a bit like an awkward dating profile! I think I'm a pretty open book on stage, so despite the layers of costume, make-up and characterization, that's probably where you'll find the most telling clues as to who I am.

----------.

This interview is also featured online at Operalively.com, with complete artistic biography, discography, pictures, and video clips. Type the following URL on your browser:

http://operalively.com/forums/content.php/977-The-Exclusive-Opera-Lively-Interview-with-Tim-Mead-countertenor.

Tammy Coil

Tammy Coil, mezzo-soprano, sang the double role of Angel 2, and Marie, in the US premiere of *Written in Skin* in Tanglewood. She is the Eunice Alberts and Adelle Alberts Vocal Studies Fellow at Tanglewood Music Center.

The New York Times said of the young singer that she performed in *Written on Skin* with "a vibrant voice," and the excellent critic Anne Midgette from the Washington Post called her singing "with engagement and amber warmth."

Luiz Gazzola for Opera Lively - You've just performed in the US premiere of George Benjamin's masterpiece Written on Skin at Tanglewood Music Center on August 12, 2013. Were you aware of this opera's enormous success in Europe? When and how did you get to know the piece for the first time? And how did the rehearsal process go? Was your role hard to learn?

Tammy Coil - I had heard that it was very well received in Europe and the buzz circulating around those initial performances really peaked my curiosity as to what I would discover in learning and performing the piece. I heard about the piece in late 2012 through colleagues, friends, and people in the music business. I began my own work on the piece in the spring of 2013 after being assigned to the project at Tanglewood, and before arriving there as a fellow. I was sent a musical score and began preparing the score by reading the story and the libretto. I began by speaking the text, to learn the rhythm of my part. I then added pitches. Adding the piano part was the next step and took a lot of patience and time because the vocal line is almost never doubled with the orchestra. The next step was adding other singers into the scene. This added new challenges in finding your own pitch and counting your rhythm against a colleague who had different rhythms in different meters simultaneously.

OL - *Written on Skin* is being heralded as the best opera written in the last 20 to 50 years, depending on the source. What is your opinion of the piece? What do you most like about it?

TC - *Written on Skin* is a work of genius. Its complexity is in every fiber of each artistic and creative choice on the page. There is not a moment, musically or otherwise, that is not completely cherished and represented, turned over and examined for all of its possible beauty or meaning. This piece is like looking into a kaleidoscope that is constantly changing and seeing the intricacies and shards of human emotion and musical expression. Its beauty and ferocity are so delicate and passionate all at once! It is poignant and heavy, deep and eternal. It is a masterpiece. I particularly like the specificity of the orchestral writing and the huge chances he makes the singers take vocally and emotionally. It requires total commitment.

OL - How were you picked to sing your part?

TC - I auditioned for Tanglewood and had attended the year before. The staff knew my voice and my capabilities as a singer and felt I would be a good fit.

OL - How vocally challenging is your part? Please describe specifically what was hard about this sing.

TC - My part is very difficult rhythmically and requires use of chest voice in a courageous way. The meter changes in almost every bar and no other instrument plays along with you while you are singing. You must find your pitch by hearing intervals in your head, silently, before you begin, either from a piece of the orchestra or from another singer. The use of chest voice was also a bit difficult to maneuver because it switched between my head register and chest register dramatically.

OL - The world premiere in Aix-en-Provence and the Royal Opera House Covent Garden run had an outstanding cast. The fully staged performance is available for streaming on MediciTV.com, and the opera has been released on CD. Have you watched it or listened to it as part of your preparation? Was it intimidating to tackle a work that has been so sublimely sung by some of the best artists in the business, for whom George Benjamin specifically wrote the vocal lines, taking into consideration the capabilities of their voices? Was it hard to adapt your own voice to this performer-specific vocal writing?

TC - I did not watch the performance because I did not want to be intimidated and have the only picture of the piece in my mind be of that performance. I wanted to let my imagination work for my character and the piece and not relate it to a specific performance. I did not want to imitate what they had done. Most every piece we sing was written originally for someone else, so I thought of it like any other work. I tried to bring my own unique qualities to the piece and trust that Mr. Benjamin would tell me what he needed and wanted from me.

OL - Please tell me about how you read the psychology of your character.

TC - I believe the Angels are a like a Greek Chorus. They represent social commentary for the time and act as a guide for the audience. Marie, Agnes's sister, cares about her sister and is unhappy with what is happening within her sister's household. She is in a marriage with John, and is the more dominant figure in that relationship. She does not like the Protector and his control over her sister. I don't believe Marie would ever actually have any actual relationship with the Boy; making the fantasy scene a true fantasy.

OL - How was for you the opportunity to work with George Benjamin in preparation for the performance? What kind of coaching or advice did he provide?

TC - Working with George Benjamin was a great honor and opportunity. His ability to hear every instrument and how they should all connect together was incredible. He is very precise and meticulous in his work with each individual. He expects a lot but is very kind and helpful in finding the best way to achieve optimum results. I loved working with him and wanted to perform with the highest level of excellence. Specifically, he helped one find a pitch by helping you hear specific instruments in the orchestra, he also was encouraging when you were able to make a correction. He also gave very vivid imagery for the colors and dynamics that he wanted.

OL - How do you think you did? Would you do anything different, given a second chance?

TC - I think that I performed well. If I had the awesome opportunity to perform the role again, I would be excited to feel more confident with the music so I could, in turn, be even more assured vocally. There is so much to discover and color in each part. The layers one can pull back seem endless. I would love the chance to sing the role again, so I could discover more and more and reveal more color and depth into my own performance.

OL - *Written on Skin* given its astounding quality in all aspects of it - music, libretto, and theatrical impact - is likely to survive the test of time and become an opera that will be remembered in the next few decades and even centuries. Having participated of the US premiere somehow writes your name in the history books of opera. How special was that, and how did you feel about it?

TC - *Written on Skin* should stand the test of time for a multitude of reasons. It is such a culmination of music and composition while at the same time being completely brand new and original! I feel very honored to have been a part of the American premiere. I am excited to see where this piece will go and so happy to have had an important part of its continued performance and expansion.

OL - How is this opportunity that you had, likely to influence your career from this point on? Did it wet your appetite for contemporary opera? What are some of your next projects?

TC - I enjoyed working on the piece very much. It was among the few contemporary operas I have ever worked on and left me excited to try new pieces. I realized how much more I am capable of and how much broader the language of opera can be. I accepted a contract premiering two new operas this fall featuring micro-tones due to the success of *Written on Skin* and my work at Tanglewood and with George Benjamin.

I am so happy to have had this incredible opportunity. I know for certain I am better-rounded, more eager, more creative, more courageous singer as a result of performing this incredible work of art. Maestro Benjamin is a truly amazing man and composer and I am so thankful for my time with him and with this score! I hope that I have the opportunity to live in his richly woven musical world again soon.

This interview is also featured online on Operalivey.com with artistic biography and pictures. Type the following URL on your browser:

http://operalively.com/forums/content.php/889-The-
Exclusive-Opera-Lively-short-Interview-with-Tammy-
Coil-Marie-in-Written-on-Skin.

Chapter Eight - The Opera in the Opera House

Interview with Stage Director Katie Mitchell

Ms. Mitchell directed the world premiere staging in Aix-en-Provence and many subsequent runs in other houses. She granted this exclusive interview to Opera Lively.

Born Katrina Jane Mitchell on September 23, 1964, she was raised in Hermitage, Berkshire, and studied English at Magdalen College, Oxford. She started her career at King's Head Theater in London, then became an assistant director at The Royal Shakespeare Company. She was granted the Evening Star award for Best Director in 1996 for her production of *The Phoenician Women* for the RSC. Operatic credits included work at the Salzburg Festival, ENO, and the Royal Opera House. She is scheduled to direct *Così fan Tutte* at the Met in the near future. Author Martin Crimp and designer Vicki Mortimer are frequent collaborators. She's been heralded as ""the closest thing the British theater has to an auteur" (The Independent, London, 17 April 2008). She was appointed Officer of the Order of the British Empire in 2009.

Some of the operas she has directed include: *Don Giovanni, Jenufa, Kat'a Kabanova, Idomeneo, and Written on Skin.*

Luiz Gazzola for Opera Lively - Please describe to us how you first heard of *Written on Skin* and how the author and composer selected you to direct the world premiere in Aix-en-Provence. Most likely it stems from your previous collaborations with Martin Crimp, I'd assume (you directed his *The Country*, his *Attempts on Her Life*, and his *The City*, before tackling *Written on Skin*), but please correct me if I'm wrong and elaborate on the seeds that led to this project. In which point of the project did you jump in? Did you have the opportunity to give input during the creation of the piece itself, or did you receive a completely finished product to work with?

Katie Mitchell - I was asked to direct the opera relatively late on in the process as Luc Bondy had to withdraw due to new pressures with his job at The Odeon. I had worked of over a decade with Martin Crimp. I directed *The Country*, The *City, Face to The Wall*, and *Attempts on Her Life*, twice (at the Royal National Theatre and also at the Piccolo Theater in Milan). We had also worked together on several versions of classic texts, including Chekhov's *The Seagull*, Buchner's *Pains of Youth* and Genet's *The Maids*. The invitation to direct *Written on Skin* was in one sense a natural extension of my collaboration with Martin and of course this relationship was my primary point of contact with the opera. It was through Martin that I had initially met George a year or so earlier and been introduced to his music *('Into the Little Hill')*. Luc had worked alongside George and Martin from the beginning, especially in the area of the casting which was already decided by the time I came on board. So I joined the process after all the key decisions had been made about the libretto, the cast. George was in the middle of finishing the arduous task of composition. It was clear that my work would focus on finding dynamic staging solutions to the musical and dramatic decisions already made by George and Martin. This was a thrilling proposition.

OL - Please describe the concept you used for the piece. I must say that you and designer Vicki Mortimer put together a truly brilliant staging, with the simultaneous rooms -- the modern/sleek look for the angels and the ancient-looking room for the characters. What were your first ideas on how to stage the piece, and how did they develop?

KM - The main challenge for Vicki and I was to create two distinct worlds, one for the angels and one for the characters in the middle age narrative. It was clear from the libretto that the angels occupied a post-war modern time period and that the characters of Agnès, The Protector and The Boy were firmly rooted in their historical period. Initially this seemed a contradiction that we couldn't really resolve in one overarching world. The breakthrough was when we realized that we could have a modern and an old world simultaneously on stage with Angel One acting as the bridge between the two worlds. After we had come to this conclusion we then worked of making the two worlds as different as possible in terms of architecture, color, texture, and lighting. The world of the angels was contemporary, blue, stark, forensic, and windowless. The world of Agnès and The Protector was warm, crumbling, flooded with light through windows, painterly.

OL - *Written on Skin* is a powerful work. I believe it has enduring power and will be talked about up to the next century and beyond, conferring some immortality of sorts to the people who first created it including the composer, the author, the singers, and yourself, which must be neat. What have you experienced as an artist when you first read the text and heard the music?

KM - I was bowled over by the power of the libretto when I first read it. I didn't really fully grasp the power of the music until I heard the singers together with the full orchestra at the Sitzprobe. By that point I had directed the whole show listening to a piano reduction supplemented with George's fantastic annotations in my score (describing the sound of the orchestra bar by bar). However nothing could have prepared me for the overwhelming power of the composition when the orchestra and singers came together. It was an emotional moment all round, and the brilliance of the composition was palpable for everyone.

OL - Were you anticipating this much success? How do you feel it will survive over time?

KM - The opera is a masterpiece, no one doubts that. It will stand the test of time.

OL - I couldn't agree more. What is your opinion of the role of the Angels and their views on humankind? They issue some rather interesting statements, like a Greek chorus.

KM - The Angels act as a kind of chorus but they are also participants in the main scenes – Angel One plays The Boy and Angels Two and Three play Marie and her husband. This is what makes their function distinct from that of a Greek chorus. They comment and participate. Their views on humankind are dark, despairing and are very much connected to the philosophy about violence emerging from Post-War writers like Walter Benjamin and Hannah Arendt.

OL - I'd like to collect your take on whether or not there is erotic tension between The Protector and The Boy as well – most notably in scene XIII - I asked the singers the same question and collected some interesting answers, so now I'd love to hear your opinion on this as well.

KM - An indirect influence on the composition for Martin was the film *Theorem* by Pasolini. It tells the story of a young man entering a middle-class conventional home and having an affair with everyone in the house: husband, wife, son, daughter, and maid. It's a very powerful film. I always understood that there was a connection between the character of The Boy in the opera and the young man in the Pasolini film in the sense that the new person (The Boy) threatens (and attracts) both Agnès and The Protector sexually. From George's point of view this was born out by the orchestration for the moment where the kiss happened between The Boy and The Protector in the production. The manifestation of attraction between the two of them was Martin and George's wish for this moment.

OL - In terms of artistic ownership of the project, how were your interactions with Mr. Crimp and Mr. Benjamin during the push to create the world premiere? I'd assume that there might be an issue (not necessary conflictual) of whose "baby" this is, when the director is tackling the work of living people being staged for the first time. This overlaps a bit with my first question but I guess that question was focused on the origin of the work, while once it's all said and done and the opera exists in paper, now it's a question of staging it, and I wonder if at the point the director takes more ownership and the author and composer sit back.

KM - My interactions with Martin and George were always clear and uncomplicated. For me the text and music were the heart of the matter and Martin and George were the primary artists. Mine was a happy secondary role – and the work I did was to support what they had both written. Practically in rehearsals Martin acted as a discreet dramaturg, guiding and giving feedback on the directing choices I was making and George focused almost exclusively on the music.

OL - And what about the singers? What advice did you have for them, and vice-versa, did you fell that you learned from them, and did you take input from them in ways that altered your directorial guidance?

KM - I worked collaboratively with the singers, integrating their ideas as much as was possible. For example, the dance skills of Barbara helped us generate the ideas of the slow motion together with the associate director Ben Davies – for example with the slow motion movement of Agnès right at the end of the opera. The insights that the singers had into the characters would always be a shaping factor of any new opera and the fact that the opera had not been done before meant that the singers did not have the shadows of other interpretations cast over their work.

OL - Are there interesting memories to tell us about the opening night in the world premiere? Do you typically relax and sit back, or are you nervous when the time for the first performance comes?

KM - By the time the first night comes my work is done and it is now over to the singers to deepen and evolve the production – and of course the conductor!

OL - The same extremely successful staging of *Written on Skin* has been revived numerous times by now, and the opera has received new productions as well. Now, with some distance between you and your work, what would you change, if anything? Have you made changes to your staging in subsequent revivals?

KM - I wouldn't want to change a thing in the production; it is all held together in a very fragile way and any changes could end up unravelling the whole concept. The music also has so many vocal demands and the staging is very much built around those demands so any staging changes would have negative repercussions on the music (which would not be a good thing).

OL - *Written on Skin* has scenes of striking eroticism, without, well, showing any skin (pun intended), in your staging. I thought it was masterfully done. Any comments on this?

KM - I was very keen to ensure that the eroticism in the story and the music was presented in a way that was true to female experience. One of the main challenges was to present a female orgasm without cheap nudity or penetrative sex scenes. I worked very closely with performers to find a subtle solution which they achieved beautifully in the production.

Complete Performance History

Written on Skin is one of the most successful contemporary operas in the last fifty years. In the summer of 2015 it will have clocked more performances than *Peter Grimes* over the same three-year period. In addition to the four performances during the world premiere run at the Grand Théâtre de Provence in Aix-en-Provence, France, on July 7-9-11-14, 2012, which got Medici TV broadcast and subsequent pay-per-view online streaming, and was recorded on CD, subsequent significant productions and broadcasts have included:

De Nederlandse Opera, Het Muziektheater, Amsterdam, Netherlands - October 6-9-11-14-17-21-23, 2012.

Théâtre du Capitole in Toulouse, France - November 23-25-27-30, 2012.

BBC Radio 3 broadcast, United Kingdom, March 2, 2013.

Royal Opera House Covent Garden, London, United Kingdom - March 8-11-16-18-22, 2013, coming back in 2017, and recorded on DVD and Blu-ray Disc.

Maggio Musicale in Florence, Italy - was scheduled for late May/Early June 2013, has been postponed indefinitely.

Wiener Festwochen (Theater an der Wien), Vienna, Austria - June 14-16-17, 2013.

BBC 4 Broadcast, United Kingdom, June 28, 2013.

Bayerisches Staatsoper, Munich, Germany - July 23-25-27, 2013.

Tanglewood Festival - U.S. premiere, concert performance, August 12, 2013 in Tanglewood, Massachusetts, USA (details and full review below).

UGC Cine Cité, Strasbourg, France – cinema screening, September 9, 2013.

L'Opéra-Comique, Paris, France - November 16-18-19, 2013.

Opernhaus, Bonn, Germany – September 29, October 4-20-26, November 17-28, December 6, 2013.

Fundação Calouste Gulbenkian, Lisbon, Portugal – May 22, 2014.

Grosses Haus, Landesthater, Detmold, Germany – April 11-16-27, May 3-24, 2014.

In total, 42 performances in 11 cities and 7 countries, with 1 online broadcast, 1 TV broadcast, 1 Radio broadcast, and 1 cinema broadcast, in addition to 1 CD, 1 DVD, and 1 Blu-ray Disc recordings – extraordinary for a contemporary opera!

Upcoming Performances (as of press time):

To the impressive totals above, future firmly scheduled runs are adding 5 more cities, 4 more countries, and 17 more performances plus some more in London.

The opera will be fully staged in New York City on August 11, 13, and 15, 2015 – Mostly Mozart Festival, Lincoln Center, Koch Theater, with the Mahler Chamber Orchestra conducted by Alan Gilbert, and Barbara Hannigan, Christopher Purves, and Tim Mead. Katie Mitchell directs, and the sets are the same as the Aix-en-Provence world premiere.

It will be revived at the Royal Opera House, Covent Garden, in 2017 – dates and details to be announced.

The Royal Swedish Opera in co-production with Landestheater Detmold, Stockholm, Sweden, country premiere. Dates: 24, 27 January, 1(m), 4, 12, 18, 22(m) February 2015. Singers: Agnès, Elin Rombo; Angel 2/Marie, Susann Vegh; Angel 3/John, Daniel Ralphsson; other roles to be announced. Conductor: Lawrence Rennes; Director: Kay Metzger; Set Designs and Costumes: Petra Mollerus; Lighting: Kay Metzger/Petra Mollerus.

Roy Thomson Hall, Toronto, Ontario, Canada, country premiere. On Saturday 7 March 2015 at 19:30, in concert. Toronto Symphony Orchestra conducted by George Benjamin. Singers: Agnès, Barbara Hannigan. Marie/Angel 2, Krisztina Szabó. John/Angel 3, Isaiah Bell. The Protector, Christopher Purves. The Boy/Angel 1, Iestyn Davies.

Gross Haus des Theaters St. Gallen, in St. Gallen, Switzerland. Dates: 2, 6, 9, 17(m) May, 5 June 2015. Singers: The Protector, Jordan Shanahan; Agnès, Evelyn Pollock; Angel 1 - The Boy, Benno Schachtner; Angel 2 – Marie, Theresa Holzhauser; Angel 3 – John, Nik Kevin Koch. Conductor: Otto Tausk; Director: Nicola Raab; Set Designs: Mirella Weingarten; Costumes: Mirella Weingarten; Lighting: Andreas Enzler.

Teatro Real, Madrid, Spain, March 17, 2016. Singers: The Protector, Christopher Purves; Agnès, Barbara Hannigan; Angel 1 - The Boy, Tim Mead; Angel 2 – Marie, Victoria Simmonds; Angel 3 – John, Robert Murray. Conductor: George Benjamin.

According to George Benjamin himself who said so to Opera Lively, beyond this list there are further planned concert or staged performances ahead in the USA, Canada, Brazil, Japan, Germany, Austria, Netherlands, Spain, and the UK, but sadly there is still no good news in reference to the Italian premiere.

The World Premiere - Review

These are fragments of Opera Lively's original review of the premiere. While it will be repetitious because some of what is here has been said elsewhere in this book, there is a freshness of the surprise the work provoked in the mind of this writer, which might be interesting to express:

Aix-en-Provence, July 7-9-11-14, 2012:

Mahler Chamber Orchestra conducted by George Benjamin

Katie Mitchell - stage director
Vicki Mortimer - costume designer, scenography
Jon Clark - lighting
Corentin Leconte - movie director

Cast:

Christopher Purves (The Protector)
Barbara Hannigan (Agnès)
Bejun Mehta (Angel 1 – The Boy)
Victoria Simmonds (Angel 2 – Marie)
Allan Clayton (Angel 3 – John)

Duration : 01 h 36 min
Location : Grand Théâtre de Provence (Aix-en-Provence, France)
Production : © Bel Air Media / Festival d'Aix-en-Provence

Orchestral parts and accompaniments are beautiful and atmospheric, the vocal lines are compelling and precise, and very well situated in relationship with the instrumental music. Pace is great, and the narrative technique is exquisite (characters refer to the action in third person as narrators then execute the action and continue to sing about the action as characters, impacting on the telling of the story an ethereal quality and intensifying the emotional impact - like watching a train wreck about to happen and having to go through the moves anyway while being the passengers at the same time).

The impression of excellence is enhanced by the fabulous concept of the setting (with the modern-looking rooms being the realm of the angels who observe the events and send in the characters to act them out) while the period-looking room gets the main action. Stage direction is precise with rather perfect blocking that explores the relative spatial position of the characters in clear relationship to the text (e.g. the wife moving to the edge of the set when the two men are talking about her as if she is an object, or the slow-motion time-standing-still final scene, etc.). The dynamic use of the various spaces delineated by the two-story sets is masterful.

Then, we get a truly outstanding cast. The three main characters look their parts, including the very attractive Barbara Hannigan, act their roles with rare intensity, and sing divinely.

What else one would want? A high-quality piece put together by a smart stage director, with a high-quality cast. The composer himself conducts, therefore adding to the precision of the proceedings, and the orchestra reacts beautifully.

We are in for a treat. This is contemporary opera at its best, and is on the same level of quality of *Luce mie traditrici* and *L'Amour de Loin*.

Gorgeous! And people still think that opera is dead! This one will survive the test of time.

I need to mention as well that lighting is one of the most effective I've seen - with the rooms lighting up or darkening down as the action progresses, spots being lit in alternation, blue colors setting the mood, and so forth.

The text is very poetic and with good literary quality. This is a contemporary *Pelléas et Mélisande*, my friends.

The last scene of the first act is extremely sensual. This director teaches a lesson to the Regie folks who feel that they need to put nudity on stage. There is no nudity, but the eroticism is devastating.

Part two - a roller-coaster of psychological drama. Very intense! One of the most interesting depictions of jealousy in opera; it's Otello-grade, and it addresses it from multiple standpoints (including some homo-erotic tones). The layers in the libretto deepen considerably as opposed to the first part. The pace is hectic. It's a shorter part but a lot happens in the psychological space. The vocal music suffers a little (there is a lot of declamation and yelling and the singers seem to be a bit fatigued - Mr. Purves loses volume a bit, and Ms. Hannigan almost gets hoarse). I don't blame the poor singers; this is very difficult to sing. The orchestral accompaniment gets percussion and harsh brass punctuating the intensity of the drama. This part two works a bit as stage play, but again, it's not really a problem, because that's what the composer and librettist clearly tried to accomplish here: the heightening of the psychological tension to almost unbearable levels. Eroticism exists as well but becomes more cruel than romantic. Again, wow! What an opera!

In time, the two comprimario roles are correctly done, especially by Ms. Simmonds. There are also four silent roles (actors who are additional angels). In summary, it's all perfect.

I have to brace for the conclusion. The public attending the premiere needs a break to fan themselves a bit. Incredible!

Part 3 recovers the orchestral beauty and the exquisite singing. Mr. Mehta remains perfect in all three parts, both in acting and in voice. Part 3 is more contemplative, as if the damage has all been done already in part 2 and we're just moving in a daze to the inevitable conclusion. This is enhanced by the stage direction by making the actors and singers move in slow motion in the astonishing final scene.

Well-deserved standing ovation greets the cast, the librettist, and the composer / conductor at the end.

Simply outstanding. I believe this to be in the top three of all contemporary operas I've ever seen, and like I said, one of the best of all time, period (as in, top 20). I couldn't more highly recommend this, and I believe that even people unfamiliar with contemporary classical music will appreciate this, and will actually want to see more works of this kind. Admirable. Bravo, Mr. Benjamin and Mr. Crimp (and hats off to Ms. Mitchell as well).

The United States Premiere at Tanglewood

Tanglewood, Massachusetts, August 12, 2013

US Premiere: Florence Gould Auditorium, Seiji Ozawa Hall - August 12, 2013 (this review is of this performance)

Tanglewood Music Center of the Boston Symphony Orchestra
Festival of Contemporary Music 2013
Concert Performance, sung in English, with English supertitles

Tanglewood Music Center Orchestra
Conductor: George Benjamin

Cast
Agnès: Lauren Snouffer, soprano
Protector: Evan Hughes, bass-baritone (guest artist)
Angel 1/Boy: Augustine Mercante, countertenor
Angel 2/Marie: Tammy Coil, mezzo-soprano
Angel 3/John: Isaiah Bell, tenor

What event would qualify as the most important operatic happening of the 2013-2014 season in the United States? Maybe the world premiere of Oscar in Santa Fe? No. The opera is good, but not great. The Metropolitan Opera opening night featuring *Eugene Onegin* with Anna Netrebko? Hardly. Similar occasions happen year after year. The various performances of operas by Britten, Verdi, and Wagner to celebrate these composers centennial and bicentennials? There is nothing unique about them – they have happened all over the world.

I'd rather say, the US premiere of the most sublime opera composed in the last several decades, *Written on Skin* by George Benjamin, conducted by the composer himself. Is it too bold a claim to make? Not at all. Let us think about it for a moment. Wouldn't you all agree that the top moment of the 1910-1911 season was the world premiere of Puccini's *La Fanciulla del West* at the Metropolitan Opera? Well, even though the conductor was none less than Arturo Toscanini, it wasn't Puccini himself. Now, when we look back at the 20th century, there aren't many opera lovers and scholars who wouldn't list Puccini as belonging to a handful of the best composers of the century - together with a few others like Richard Strauss, Benjamin Britten, Alban Berg, Stravinsky...

I am absolutely convinced that music lovers and scholars in the 22nd century will look back at the 21st century and list George Benjamin among a similar handful of the best composers of the century, while heralding *Written on Skin* as the first true masterpiece of the century. It boasts an inventive score of the highest degree of precision and beautiful tone-painting, there is great pace and dramatic impact, its libretto is terrific and with enormous literary value... in summary, this opera is just perfect. George's piece is by far the most impressive work composed in this century, miles ahead of the competition. I'd say that *L'Amour de Loin* by Saariaho might compete, but it premiered in the very last year of the 20th century. However, Ms. Saariaho continues to compose, and she will likely qualify with Benjamin in that select list of best 21st century opera composers. Another one would have been Sciarrino's *Luci mie traditrici*. Alas, it was composed in 1998. Similarly, since Mr. Sciarrino is also alive and active, he'll be keeping company with Saariaho and Benjamin. Then, we'll see. Other candidates have never impressed me as much. Don't read me wrong, there are plenty of talented composers around, and worthy contemporary operas - just, not as good as *Written on Skin.*

Lauren Snouffer, Evan Hughes, Augustine Mercante, Evan Hughes, Isaiah Bell, and George Benjamin – photo credit Opera Lively

Rest assured that I'm not alone in this assessment. Literally dozens of reviewers from all sorts of newspapers and magazines agree with me (Le Monde, Le Figaro, The New Yorker, The Guardian, etc.), after the opera's smashing success throughout Europe, where it has received sold out performances at prestigious houses such as the ROH Covent Garden, the Bavarian State Opera in Munich, the DNO in Amsterdam, and the Theater an den Wien in Vienna, with an upcoming performance scheduled for

L'Opéra-Comique in Paris (November 16-18-19, 2013), as well as a return to the Royal Opera House, and in the relatively near future, Toronto and New York. In its first 13 months of existence the opera has already received eight productions, a feat almost unheard of, in contemporary opera.

So, the most respected work of the 21st century so far (and even though the century is still young, I'm quite sure this opera will retain this title for a very long time) comes to America for the first time under the baton of the composer himself - if this doesn't qualify as the most important operatic event of the season, I don't see what else would.

Given that this performance was a single one, a privileged few snatched the seats of the sold-out Seiji Ozawa Hall in the beautiful Tanglewood campus, and witnessed history - this writer, luckily, among them, and thankfully, on the very first row, mere yards away from the composer/conductor and the soloists.

In this review, I won't be addressing the opera in detail, simply because it is not necessary to repeat it all here.

So, being brief and to the point, how was this performance, tonight? In two simple words, surprisingly good. We got young artists as instrumentalists (with a few exceptions - a more senior musician took care of the glass harmonica, given that it is difficult to find musicians who can play this exquisite instrument) - and as soloists. The original cast that premiered the work was so incredibly good - with the principal trio being made of hugely talented Bejun Mehta, Barbara Hannigan, and Christopher Purves, that I was apprehensive for the ability of these youngsters to tackle this difficult score. Besides, the productions running throughout Europe are fully staged -

and very exquisitely so - by Katie Mitchell, while the US premiere was a concert performance.

Regardless, this piece is so beautiful both in music and in text, that the concert was still a goose-bumping experience. Some unique features for me, as compared to the gorgeous full staging in Aix-en-Provence, were the opportunity to see up-close George's energetic conducting, and to listen to the glass harmonica a few yards away, as well as being able to see how each section of the orchestra produced the intriguing sounds of this outstanding score.

All five young soloists who are current Tanglewood fellows except for Evan Hughes who is former fellow, did a fabulous job. All five were good singers who delivered the vocal lines with passion, power, fury, and emotion. I am quite sure that they felt the force of this work even more than the audience. They seemed quite thrilled themselves for being part of this.

Countertenor Augustine Mercante drew the most applause from the audience, and deservedly so. He hails from Wilmington, DE, and as a 2010 Fulbright Scholar, he studied in Germany and performed with companies in Augsburg, Munich, and Nuremberg, as well as Salzburg, Austria. Currently a recipient of the 2013 Individual Artist Fellowship rom the Delaware Division of the Arts, he continues to further his education and to be involved in new projects. He sang the role of The Boy/Angel 1 with great delicacy.

Soprano Lauren Snouffer has just finished her two years as a member of the Houston Grand Opera Studio (their young artist program), and was a grand finalist of the 2012 National Council Auditions. She is scheduled to debut with the Lyric Opera of Chicago and other companies. Her Agnès was defiant, fierce, and she did well with the wide vocal range of the role for the most part, in spite of a bit of vocal fatigue at the very end.

Our Protector was Evan Hughes, a guest at Tanglewood, given that he is currently a member of the Metropolitan Opera's Lindemann Young Artist Development Program. He has already been at the Met's main stage in *La Rondine*. He is a former Tanglewood fellow, has performed in Don Giovanni under James Levine, and has sung at Carnegie Hall already. Mr. Hughes tonight had very clear diction and good acting with the voice.

Tammy Coil, a Juilliard alumna who has had roles at Santa Fe Opera, Opera Theater of St. Louis, and Opera Philadelphia among others, did well in the comprimario part of Marie/Angel 2.

Canadian tenor Isaiah Bell was able to shine even though his part is also small (Angel 3/John). His voice has a beautiful timbre and is very well projected. He has done good work with prestigious conductors such as Kent Nagano and Yannick Nézet-Séguin with various Canadian orchestras and opera companies, and has sung the difficult *Winterreise* already.

I thought that the young instrumentalists in the orchestra did a superb job. Transitions were smooth, and the dynamics were rather perfect, from the pianissimo in the strings during the most intimate moments, to the loud percussion during the hectic events of part 3.

Absent but present through his text was the great Martin Crimp. The hall provided two large screen TV monitors on each side of the orchestra, with the supertitles. An opera that opens like this gives you already a jolt in your spine:

Strip the cities of brick, dismantle them.

Strip out the wires and cover the land with grass.
Force chrome and aluminum back into the earth.
Cancel all flights from the international airports -
And people the sky with angels.
Erase the Saturday car-park from the marketplace,
rub out the white lines:
make way for the wild primrose
and slow torture of criminals.
Shatter the printing-press.
Make each new book a precious object written on skin.
Fade out the living:
snap back the dead to life.

George Benjamin greeting the orchestra – photo credit Opera Lively

To make this evening of superlative music even more satisfying, I had the immense pleasure of meeting George Benjamin in person, backstage. I was touched with the fact that he thanked Opera Lively for all the support we've been giving him. With his well-known modesty and grace, the brilliant composer said I was being silly, when I told him that meeting him was a pleasure similar to what I imagine other opera lovers have experienced in the past when they met Verdi and Puccini. Well, his teacher Olivier Messiaen used to compare him to Mozart, so, I can't be too out of line...

General Index

In the next few pages the reader will find a general index with names of singers, conductors, stage directors, composers, writers, some orchestras and opera houses, and opera titles.

Names of persons and titles are alphabetized respectively by first name and first letter of the title in original language (articles do count). Many famous composers, painters, and writers are only listed by last name. In doubt, look up alphabetization by both first and last names.

Acis and Galatea, 130

Adelina Patti, 109

Admeto, 148, 149, 152

Aix-en-Provence, ii, 2, 19, 97, 98, 99, 100, 108, 120, 124, 127, 129, 138, 160, 164, 165, 171, 172, 174, 182

Akhnaten, 153

Alcina, 130

Alexander Goehr, 24

Alfred Deller, 147

Alice in Wonderland, 119

Allan Clayton, 18, 98, 100, 174

Andreas Jören, 97

Andreas Scholl, 146, 148

Anna Netrebko, 178

Anna Werle, 98

Anthony Negus, 132

Anu Komsi, 12, 26

Arturo Toscanini, 179

Audun Iversen, 112

Augustine Mercante, 97, 178, 180, 182

Axel Köhler, 148

Bach, 128, 130, 146, 148

Barbara Hannigan, vi, 4, 18, 95, 96, 104, 105, 131, 139, 172, 173, 174, 175, 181

Bejun Mehta, 18, 97, 100, 112, 138, 174, 181

Ben Davies, 169

Berg, 10, 179

Berlin Philharmonic, 25, 108, 119

Bernard Foccroulle, 14, 36, 73

Bernhard Landauer, 95, 97

Birtwistle, 142

Boccaccio, 2, 68

Brahms, 148

Britten, 10, 121, 156, 178, 179

Cantos, 68

Cavalli, 145, 152

Charles Brett, 147

Christian Curnyn, 154

Christophe Dumaux, 147

Christopher Purves, vi, 4, 18, 95, 97, 100, 112, 124, 125, 172, 173, 174, 181

Christopher Wintle, 103

Concertgebouw, 25, 120, 154

Così fan Tutte, 165

Curlew River, 156

Daniel Ralphsson, 95, 98, 173

Das Rheingold, 132

David Daniels, 147, 148

David McVicar, 154

Debussy, 10, 28, 148

Decameron, 68

Dietrich Henschel, 27

Domique Visse, 147

Donizetti, 15

Doris Dörrie, 148

Dowland, 147

Dusapin, 118

Dutilleux, 120

Elin Rombo, 95, 96, 173

Ercole Amante, 145, 151, 152

Esa-Pekka Salonen, 120

Eugene Onegin, 178

Evan Hughes, 97, 178, 180, 182, 183

Evellyn Pollock, 96

Evez Abdulla, 97

Ezra Pound, 68

Faber Music, ii, vi, 3, 30, 36, 80, 99

Faure, 148

Festival d'Aix-en-Provence, 36, 73

Ford Madox Ford, 68

Francesco Conti, 145

George Benjamin, ii, iii, vi, 1, 7, 8, 9, 24, 25, 27, 72, 75, 79, 85, 100, 103, 105, 109, 158, 160, 161, 162, 173, 174, 178, 179, 180, 184

Gerald Barry, 119

Gianni Schicchi, 21

Giulio Cesare, 154

Glass, 153

Glyndebourne, 147, 154

Grisey, 25

Guillem de Cabestaing, 2

Handel, 107, 128, 130, 132, 142, 144, 145, 146, 148, 149, 152

Hannah Arendt, 168

Hans Abrahamsen, 22, 119

Hilary Summers, 12, 26

Iestyn Davies, 97, 112, 173

Into the Little Hill, 3, 10, 12, 13, 17, 25, 29, 76, 166

Isaiah Bell, 98, 173, 178, 180, 183

Jean Francois Sivadier, 151

Jeremy Carpenter, 95, 97

Jon Clark, 103, 174

Jordan Shanahan, 97, 173

Julian Anderson, 22

Kathleen Kelly, 132

Katie Mitchell, vi, 4, 17, 18, 19, 92, 103, 106, 112, 164, 165, 172, 174, 182

Kent Nagano, 27, 183

Krysztof Warlikowski, 107, 113

L'Incoronazione di Poppea, 150

L'Issipile, 145

L'Olympiade, 145

La Calisto, 145

La Fanciulla del West, 179

L'Amour de Loin, 176, 179

Lauren Snouffer, 96, 178, 180, 182

Laurence Dreyfus, 13

Lawrence Zazzo, 147

Lee Blakely, 153

Les Illuminations, 121

Les Troyens, ii, 3, 193

Ligeti, 10, 25, 119

Luce mie traditrici, 176

Lucia di Lammermoor, 15

Lulu, 107, 108, 113

Maria Malibran, 109

Markus Gruber, 98

Martin Crimp, ii, vi, 3, 12, 13, 14, 25, 27, 30, 35, 36, 69, 70, 71, 103, 137, 165, 183

Mary Garden, 109

Metropolitan Opera, 178, 179, 183, 193

Michael Chance, 147

Michael Waldman, 23

Miriam Clark, 96

Monteverdi, 142, 145, 151, 193

Mozart, 11, 107, 124, 132, 134, 172, 184

New York Philharmonic, 141

Nigel Lowrey, 153

Nik Kevin Koch, 98, 173

Ole Anders Tandberg, 150

Oliver Knussen, 22, 27

Olivier Messiaen, 10, 24, 184

Oscar, 118, 178

Ozawa Hall, 20, 178, 181

Pasolini, 168

Passion, 118, 130

Pelléas et Mélisande, 10, 25, 130

Peter Grimes, 2, 171

Philip Ledger, 156

Philippe Jaroussky, 148

Pierre Boulez, 10

Provence, 68

Puccini, 179, 184

Purcell, 10

Rebecca Jo Loeb, 98, 100

Riccardo Primo, 153

Richard Strauss, 179

Robert Johnson, 147

Robin Blaze, 147

Royal Opera House, ii, 21, 28, 29, 36, 76, 95, 97, 98, 99, 103, 160, 164, 171, 172, 181

Saariaho, 179

San Giovanni Battista, 156

Sciarrino, 10, 28, 179

Simon Holt, 22

Stendhal, 2

Stradella, 156

Stravinsky, 179

Susan Végh, 98

Susanne Blattert, 98

Tamás Tarjányi, 98

Tammy Coil, 4, 98, 157, 158, 178, 183

Tanglewood, 4, 20, 158, 159, 162, 171, 178, 181, 182, 183

Terry Wey, 97

The Bitter Tears of Petra von Kant, 119

The Importance of Being Ernest, 119

The Minotaur, 142, 143

The Rise of Spinoza, 154

The Stronger, 119

Theo Loevendie, 154

Theorem, 168

Theresa Holzhauser, 98, 173

Tim Mead, vi, 4, 112, 134, 172

Tristan Murail, 22

Unsuk Chin, 22, 25, 193

Vera-Lotte Böcker, 96

Verdi, 132, 178, 184

Vicki Mortimer, 103, 165, 166, 174

Victoria Simmonds, 18, 98, 103, 174

Vivaldi, 145

Wagner, 132, 178

Walter Benjamin, 168

Webern, 10

William Christie, 150

Winterreise, 183

Wolfgang Rihm, 25

Wozzeck, 128, 129

Yannick Nézet-Séguin, 120, 183

Yehudi Menuhin, 122

ABOUT THE AUTHOR

Luiz Gazzola © Opera Lively Press

Luiz Gazzola, MD, PhD, has loved opera since a lucky encounter with
Carmen decades ago. Over the years, he has explored the opera repertory
from Monteverdi to George Benjamin, taking in hundreds of recorded and
live performances (he used to live two blocks from the Metropolitan
Opera House), as well as reading widely on the subject. Opera is in Dr.
Gazzola's blood, given that he is a dual citizen of Italy and the United
States who speaks five languages. He holds the position of Chief Editor at
Opera Lively, and is the author of "Opera Lively – The Interviews,"
volumes 1 and 2, and "The Opera Lively Guides – Les Troyens" also
published by Opera Lively Press.

His passion for this fascinating art form drove him to embrace a second
career as a registered opera journalist, while remaining active as a Board
Certified Psychiatrist. Dr. Gazzola, who authored a book on Obsessive-
Compulsive Personality Disorder, is a graduate of Columbia University,
with a doctoral degree in Psychoanalysis from the University of Paris,
France. He has written articles for cultural magazines, and led a seminar
on Cinema and Psychoanalysis at Columbia University. Opera, cinema,
and literature join fine wines as his main interests together with his family
and profession. He currently lives with his wife Marta in North Carolina,
where he teaches students from Duke University. In between Psychiatry
lessons, he always makes a point of introducing opera to his students,
refusing to be discouraged by a dismal 6% conversion rate for new opera
fans among them.

CPSIA information can be obtained at www.ICGtesting.com
Printed in the USA
LVOW06s1611210715

447056LV00025B/1387/P

9 780692 379714